Pat + Karen,
May this book
richly bless you
and may God bless
your lives as you
continue on the
journey.
He is always in
control.

LESSONS FROM SAN QUENTIN

H 64741

Lessons from San Quentin

Everything I Needed to Know about Life I Learned in Prison

Bill Dallas
with George Barna

Tyndale House Publishers, Inc.
CAROL STREAM, ILLINOIS

Library of Congress Cataloging-in-Publication Data

Dallas, Bill.
    Lessons from San Quentin : everything I needed to know about life I learned in prison / Bill Dallas, with George Barna.
        p. cm.
    Includes bibliographical references.
    ISBN 978-1-4143-2656-6 (hc)
1. Dallas, Bill. 2. Christian converts—California—San Quentin—Biography.
3. Prisoners—California—San Quentin—Biography. 4. Prisoners—Religious life.
5. Success—Religious aspects—Christianity. 6. California State Prison at San Quentin.
I. Barna, George. II. Title.
    BV4935.D35A3 2009
    277.3'083092—dc22
    [B]   2008037940

Printed in the United States of America

15 14 13 12 11 10 09
  7   6   5   4   3   2   1

To Vy,

the greatest friend I ever had.

You saved my life and then taught me

how to walk.

Contents

Foreword

I believe the world can be divided into three kinds of people based on the different ways they view the difficulties of life. The first group of people feel like "it's over" before it even begins. They see all the bad things that *could* happen to them, or to their dreams or plans, so they attempt very little. They are convinced that anything they try will have a bad outcome and "will never work." So they refuse to get out of their comfort zones and, therefore, never become who they were meant to be.

The second group of people experienced such a terrible failure at some point that they came to believe "it's over." These individuals are not like the first group of people who never tried. They did try, but when they failed, they assumed the dismal outcome was a message about themselves, their dreams, and sometimes, if the failure was large enough, about life itself. They let the failure tell them, "Forget it. You will never . . ." So they came to believe that "it's over when it's over." Like the first group of people, they never became who they were meant to be. A particular failure stopped them from ever trying again.

The third group of people believe that "it's *never* over." They discover that if they have the few essential ingredients from which new life emerges, a failure or the death of any dream is never the end, but only the first step of a new beginning.

Further, they allow their painful experiences to become the crucibles within which they *do* become who they were meant to be. They are reinvented through the failure itself.

In this book, and in the story of Bill's life, we see the third kind of person emerging. We also learn the key ingredients that bring new life and a new person out of the death of an old one. We see that a bigger story looms behind whatever failure or pain we may be going through: it is the story of God, His love for us, and a future of hope, no matter where we find ourselves.

We will see that He is always there looking for us and offering us a way of redemption that will require each of us in some way to become a "new me" and to realize the promise He has for us. That is the essence of God's story, to pick us up in our failures and turn us into different people. As the apostle James tells us, when, through faith, we persevere in our trials and learn their lessons, we become "mature and complete, not lacking anything" (James 1:4). Bill shows us just how true that is, no matter what depths we may hit along the road to God's future plans for us.

Bill's story demonstrates that we do not have to be one of the first two types of people, either never trying or giving up when "it's over." He shows us that even when all seems lost, it is never really over. And if we remember that God is God, we can overcome the inertia that comes from never trying or from fearing that failure has made trying once again impossible. Bill's story reminds us that God has a bigger story and plan for all of us.

Another delightful reminder in Bill's story is that God made us as we are for a reason. The problem comes when our own weaknesses and self-destructive patterns, old-fashioned sin, and immaturity interfere with His best intentions for us. You'll read about the self-destructive patterns that contributed to Bill's downfall, yet you'll also see the tremendous strengths, gifts, and talents that made him such a successful entrepreneur early in life. Later, when God picked him up off the ground in a prison yard, He did not trash the whole person He had made, the real Bill Dallas. Instead, He refined the rough edges that were keeping Bill's gifts and talents from being realized in a truly productive way. At one time Bill's gifts, when mixed with sin and immaturity, got him into trouble. Now God has taken those same gifts of creativity, energy, and people skills, which were once manipulative and self-serving, and He has redeemed them to be used in ways that not only fulfill Bill more than he ever was fulfilled before (and without causing him to self-destruct) but that also benefit millions of people through his work with the Church Communication Network (CCN).

God will do the same for you if you let Him. He will take the real person He made you to be, with all of your gifts and talents, and He will work out the kinks that are keeping those gifts from fruition. During this process of redemption, God usually does not turn apples into oranges. More often, he turns bruised, wormy apples to red, shiny fruit that will nourish others. You do not have to fear becoming a weird, alien person if you let God work in your life. Instead, you will become more of yourself—just without the worm holes and bruises.

I remember the first time I met Bill and he convinced me to begin broadcasting with CCN. I know a deal maker when I see one, and his promotion was as deft as it gets. I suspect that the investors in his real estate ventures signed up as a result of the same art of persuasion. So the old Bill is still around, enjoying his natural bent even more than he did then, I am sure. He was not sent to wear a toga in an airport when he gave himself to God. He was sent out to be himself. The difference is that now when we partner with him, we know that we are not going to be "taken" by a manipulative deal maker but are joining hands in a mission that is motivated by a real sense of mission and a pure heart. In like fashion, if you fear that God will turn you into something you are not if you make a deeper commitment to Him, you'll discover quite the opposite: He will turn you into more of yourself, just a better version.

But as Bill also shows, that might not be exactly who you think you are now. God probably knows some things about you that you don't, like some things that you would be good at but that currently are hidden talents buried in the ground. As you'll see, Bill found out that he liked television production while in prison, not in the real estate business. Allow God to show you, even in your pain and failure, what He has for you. You might be surprised to find out that you have talents you didn't even know were there and that God has opportunities for those talents to be used if only you will lay them before Him.

I feel grateful to write the foreword to Bill's story. I remember trying to get him to tell it publicly for years, yet he did not want it to get in the way of the mission of CCN. But once he became convinced that CCN was established enough that his past would not be an obstacle and that his story might give others hope for their futures, he decided to share it. I was lucky enough to do the initial interview on a CCN broadcast when he told it publicly for the first time. I can tell you that there was a resounding chorus of tears and appreciation for his sharing what God had done for him, with resulting hope, thanksgiving, and inspiration for all who listened. I am sure you will benefit in the same way as you read his story here.

Thank you, Bill, for sharing, and as 2 Corinthians 2:14 says, "Thanks be to God, who always leads us in triumphal procession in Christ and through us spreads everywhere the fragrance of the knowledge of him." Through your story, we give Him thanks for what He has done, can do, and will do as you and others through CCN spread "the fragrance of the knowledge of him."

God Bless,
Henry Cloud, PhD
Los Angeles, 2008

Acknowledgments

I am thankful for so many people who have helped shape my life and guide my journey.

To my wife, my best friend, and my ultimate cheerleader, Bettina, thanks for putting up with me. You are my true "Sweet, Sweet." To my son, Dallas, I am so very proud to be your father, and I so much enjoy being with you. To my daughter, Amanda, your zest for life brings me great joy.

To the people—no, to my family at CCN. This is the greatest job I've ever had, and it is all because of you.

To all my ministry partners with whom I have worked over the years: Henry, John, Lee, Mark, Jim, Steve, Dennis, Gary, Roger, H. B., Tim, Les, Leslie, Joe, and Constance. I am grateful for your partnership and friendship.

To the people who showed me how to grow in Christ: Gordon, Paul, and Tony.

To the people who came alongside me to help me when I got out of prison: Dennis and Sharon, for giving me a place to stay; Toni, for all of your support; Michael, for being my friend; Ed, for giving me my first job out of prison; Reid, for helping me build the plan for CCN; and John, for backing my dreams.

To my agent, Esther, for encouraging me to write this book.

To the team at Tyndale: Jan, Doug, Nancy, Yolanda, and Sharon, for believing in this project, and especially to my editor, Lisa, for being patient with me and for adding all of the right spices and ingredients to make this book come alive.

To George, thank you for writing the book with me. I am so honored that you wanted to do it and so grateful for the excellent job that you did.

And, finally, to my ultimate small group, my brothers of San Quentin. This book is for you and because of you. You are truly the men of God, and I aspire to be like you.

Finding God in San Quentin

It's a sunny, crisp spring day. I am driving north on Highway 101, having just crossed the Golden Gate Bridge. Suddenly my destination comes into view off to the right. Looming above the San Francisco Bay is a massive compound of limestone-colored buildings surrounded by towers featuring armed guards. Here amidst the multi-million-dollar homes and scenic hills of prestigious Marin County is San Quentin State Prison.

This was the place I called home in the early 1990s while I served my sentence for a felony conviction. When I arrived as a scared and disoriented thirty-one-year-old, I knew no one there—nor did I want to. I was convinced that my being placed in San Quentin was an incredible mistake. I was also certain that if I stayed, I would die there. This was the beginning of the end for Bill Dallas.

But that was before I went through a series of dramatic encounters that completely transformed my life. Inside those enormous walls live a group of extraordinary men that I came to know and love during my time behind bars. Several of them have become like family to me, and since my parole, I have returned regularly to this imposing prison to visit them. To the surprise of my friends on the outside who know of my frequent visits, I actually feel a sense of peace and joy as I speed closer to the gated entryway of the prison.

Having spent countless hours looking with dread at those thick, unassailable walls from the inside, I have only positive feelings today as my eyes are drawn to the outer walls. My joy and calm anticipation are not because I endured the challenges of prison and now live as a free man. My happiness comes from knowing that this is the place where I learned to be a *real* man, the place where I discovered the principles that would eventually enable me to live a meaningful and successful life. I would not be the person I am today had it not been for the nurture and training I received behind those impregnable walls.

Despite its waterfront setting—situated on land whose estimated value exceeds $100 million, reputedly making it the most valuable prison in the world—San Quentin is hardly a luxury hotel for criminals. It is the oldest prison in the California state prison system, constructed back in 1852 at the tail end of the gold rush. It houses roughly five thousand convicted criminals, including the state's only male death row. It also contains the state's sole gas chamber, although that space is now used only for lethal injections.

San Quentin has a colorful history. It has been the home of such infamous inmates as Charles Manson, Sirhan Sirhan,

Richard Ramirez, and even the infamous stagecoach bandit Black Bart. Country music has a history here, too, with Merle Haggard having been on the inside for burglary. Johnny Cash, the country legend who did time in another prison, played a famous concert at San Quentin in 1969, the recording of which later became one of his best-known albums.

But the who's who list of the criminal justice system is the last thing on my mind as I approach the visitor's parking lot on this day.

I am about to be reunited with Vy Le, the Vietnamese immigrant who surrendered his life to the state police and then years later to Jesus Christ. Slight of build and always smiling, Vy became my spiritual mentor through the quiet dignity of his determination to be Christlike in a den of anger and hubris.

I know I will get my usual crushing hug from Big D, a massive African American with the most tender heart you could imagine.

If all goes well I may get to see Kevin Hagan, Binh Vong, Terry Coran, Leonard Rubio, and several others who became the community that pulled me through some of the darkest days imaginable.

Every one of these dear brothers is serving a life sentence; many of them are convicted murderers. But if the occasion ever arose, I would not hesitate to sacrifice my life for them.

My time in San Quentin produced a profound awakening in my life and changed me forever.

In a strange way, I feel as if I am home.

|||

It's always interesting for me when fellow Christians speak about their journeys with God. I've heard descriptions of the churches and Bible studies that have affected them, prayers that were answered in magnificent ways, and even times when they felt God was speaking directly to them. I can certainly relate to God's intervention, having been radically changed by the power of God through some extraordinary experiences. But my transformation didn't happen in a church auditorium or small group. It took place in a much different setting.

In much the same way that God used a prison term to capture the attention and hearts of Joseph, Daniel, and even the apostle Paul, He used my years in confinement to reshape everything about me. God can and will use any situation to mold us into the people He intends us to become—which means becoming more like His Son.

Yet even though my prison term led to a full-bore personal renaissance, I did not write this book to glorify prison life. There's not much about life behind bars that you would envy. That is, after all, the purpose of time in prison: to break you down and enable the authorities to reform you. San Quentin is not a country-club prison; it is an old, uncomfortable, remote, overcrowded, fear-inducing, spirit-breaking place. For most of the people locked within its high, thick walls, San Quentin is a place of little hope. Every day its prisoners are reminded that they have lost their most precious possessions: family, freedom, reputation, identity, and more.

Doing time in San Quentin was by far the hardest thing I have ever done. But it was also the best thing that ever happened to me, and I would not trade a single minute of that ordeal.

Looking back on my journey, it is obvious that God had to do some major reconstruction in me. My life was a wreck, but God loved me so much that He orchestrated a bizarre set of circumstances in order to get my attention and facilitate the kind of wholesale transformation I so desperately needed.

It was not until recently, as I was sharing my tale with others, that the idea of writing a book about the lessons I derived from San Quentin began to take shape. Writing such a book was a scary thought to me—much scarier than the idea of returning to the tight quarters of a prison cell. My own limitations and failings are laid bare in these pages as you join me on a return visit to some of the best and worst times of my life. You will discover all kinds of things about me that make me sick to think about now but that were the centerpiece of my life years ago.

Despite such points of discomfort and embarrassment, I am truly honored to be able to share many of the principles that I learned while incarcerated. Although these are lessons that completely changed me, I know they are neither new nor original. Indeed, Solomon observed that there is nothing new under the sun—everything old comes back in fresh ways after some time passes (Ecclesiastes 1:9-10).

So what I will be describing in this book is merely a new spin on ancient, proven truths. That's about all that any author can offer: new hope based upon foundational truths, communicated a bit differently, but drawn from the only well of profundity that we can count on, God's Word. I pray that my unusual context for grasping these truths will resonate in your heart and motivate you to rethink and redesign aspects of your life that need to be refreshed.

In essence, this is a book about being transformed by God. I had to learn the hard way that such renewal is not about what we do or accomplish. It's about who we hope to become and what we allow God to do in our minds and hearts to facilitate growth. Make no mistake about it, growth is always painful, but the only alternative is death (which, technically, is the absence of growth). Spiritual transformation is a lifelong journey, one that I am still traveling with all kinds of starts, stops, reversals, and twists. But it is a journey I would not be on had it not been for my days in San Quentin.

And if God could get ahold of and thoroughly remake me, rest assured that He can do the same thing with you! You don't have to be convicted of murder or some other horrendous crime to benefit from the lessons God taught me in prison. Maybe your battles are with drugs or alcohol. Perhaps your marriage is on the rocks or your relationship with your children has turned sour. It could be a financial situation that keeps you up at night or health problems not even of your own making.

Whatever the challenge may be, we all have prisons that separate us from the love and power of God. But He promises that if we let Him inside the walls around our minds and hearts, He will perform miracles of reconstruction, enable us to transcend our circumstances, and empower us to break through whatever is holding us back from experiencing all the joy, peace, and truth that He has in store for us.

But part of the deal is that you must be a willing partner in the process. That means not just reading a book like this, but also earnestly attempting to apply the principles that you will learn. There are no magic steps and no simple formulas. But if you devote yourself to the principles that God taught me— shards of wisdom that mirror the stories of previous hard-headed, hard-hearted men described in the Bible—then you, too, can become a new creation in Christ.

I hope that the end result will be a challenge to your character that drives you back to the Christ who has saved us from ourselves and the God who is powerful enough to transform even the most stubborn heart and ignorant mind. He will not force you to change; but if you seek His guidance and strength, He will be right there with you. I know because that is my experience with Him. It is a journey that continues to this day.

It took time behind bars for me to learn these principles. My prayer is that it will not take a sentence in San Quentin for you to "get it"—unless that is God's best plan for your life too.

CHAPTER 1

Life in the Median Strip

When I entered San Quentin for the first time, I was only thirty-one years old. Still reeling from the chain of events that had landed me there, I couldn't believe this was now my life. Numb with disbelief, I tried not to think about where I was and who I would be living with. These people were lowlifes—hard-core criminals. They were beneath me, and I couldn't believe that I would now be considered one of them.

How was this possible? How did I go from being the golden boy of the Bay Area to fresh meat in a state prison?

My life had been going great—better than great, in fact. After graduating with honors from Vanderbilt University in Tennessee, I had made my way west and learned the real estate business. By the mideighties I had joined with my business partner, Tony, and we were determined to take the San Francisco Bay area by storm.

We got off to a flying start. We put together huge deals, raising capital from investors who liked our creativity and chutzpah. Tony and I became known as the boy wonders of the Bay Area, and we reveled in that reputation. We also believed that this was only the beginning of the riches and fame that were surely in store for us.

While some people are known for being type A personalities, I was easily a type triple A. I wasn't just living in the fast lane; I was going so fast I was burning down the median strip! Life seemed to be beckoning me for greatness, and nothing was going to stop me from living what I deemed to be the good life.

While I learned to play the real estate game in the Bay Area, I also worked as a male model. The money was good, but it was the clothing and attention that really appealed to me. Once I hit it big in real estate, I wore the finest threads available. I believed that image was everything, and I was selling it big-time. Because I needed to raise megabucks for the downtown developments I was always pushing, I knew it was critical that I looked the part of the well-to-do, successful magnate. No suit was too expensive or too finely tailored for me—Hugo Boss and Armani were my favorites. Throw in some exquisite Italian loafers and a brilliant designer tie, and with my hair gelled back, I was ready for action.

In fact, action seemed to be my middle name. I was constantly entertaining women at home, in clubs, even on the job. Cocaine was my drug of choice, and I always had a designer vodka cocktail in my hand. I loved cutting through traffic in my sleek black BMW sedan on the way to business meetings or driving my gleaming black Porsche around town on weekends.

Late at night, you could find me and my high-flying entourage cruising the city, looking for the best scene. My party mates and I regularly rented stretch limos to weave through the streets in search of the hottest clubs. Sometimes we even intentionally circled a specific club, waiting for a sufficiently long line of partyers to form behind the velvet rope outside. We wanted to pull up to the carpeted entryway and make a grand entrance.

Orchestrating favorable press coverage and wrangling introductions to the most important power players in the area became our standard operating procedure.

I quickly gained insight into how the political system worked, and I began to throw fund-raisers for key city officials—not just one candidate per race, but multiple candidates—being sure to grease their palms so they would approve our real estate projects. Often, I handed out more money than could be legally donated, but I always figured out ways to skirt the laws. Such rules were merely a minor nuisance in my climb to the top of the world.

And when it was time to work the system, we worked it mercilessly. When we desperately needed to secure city funding for a $100 million development we were working on, I even dated a government official who would be influential in the decision-making process. The campaign coffers of several of the councilmen were filled, thanks to my generosity. In addition, Tony and I recruited people to pack a critical city council meeting and say great things about our proposed project. The line of "local residents" extended outside the council chambers and down the block. The chairman eventually cut the meeting short, noting that the public's overwhelming sentiment for the project could not be more obvious. The city council voted in our favor.

I was Bill Dallas, boy wonder. I had it all figured out.

III

As it turned out, there were a few things I hadn't figured out. For instance, one of the details I failed to anticipate was the real estate crash of the early nineties. When it hit, it smacked me like a two-by-four across the head. Many people were taken by surprise by this swift and deep change in the economy, but I was taken hostage.

By the spring of 1991, we had used all of the money invested in our projects to fuel our combustible lifestyle and promote other, newer projects we were setting up. The combination of out-of-control spending, not enough financial planning, and the demise of the real estate market caused us to run out of money, plain and simple. Our financial backers, some of whom were falling on tough times as well—thanks in part to my lofty promises about the returns they would be receiving— began asking about their investments, wondering why work on their projects had been halted and how they were going to fare during the real estate downturn. That's when everything started to blow up in our faces.

Our business strategy had been based on impressing people with sizzle rather than substance. We had cut corners

and manipulated every angle in an attempt to provide investors with a world-class return on their investments, which
incidentally would also have meant that *we* would be rolling
in cash as well.

But that dream was not to be. My business collapsed, and
the life I had built around it began to crash. Big-time. Our
luxurious office with its panoramic view was shut down. The
phones were turned off. I was kicked out of my penthouse, and
my prized toys—my homes and cars—were repossessed. My
friends found new parties to enjoy and more successful partyers to accompany. The man of the year quickly became a social
leper.

As if things weren't bad enough, the legal hammer began
to fall. Due to a lethal combination of ignorance and ambition, I had been handling investors' money in a way that was
apparently illegal—something called commingling of funds.
We had used money from one project to float another without
the investors' knowledge. Although my partner and I always
intended to pay back each investor after we completed our
development activity, our naive and reckless approach was still
against the law. Both the state and federal governments wound
up filing charges against me, and a drawn-out, expensive
courtroom drama began to unfold.

In the meantime, I sought any job I could get and wound
up as a salesman at Nordstrom. I think I got the job because I
had such fabulous clothing, but I wasn't much of a salesman on
the retail floor. My heart just wasn't in it. In fact, my heart was
nowhere to be found.

I was completely empty, almost numb, and had little energy for life. In the past, I had always been able to push away such feelings of emptiness with new toys, loud parties, and a lot of women. But now, without any of those things to distract me, I was faced with the fact that I didn't really like my life—or myself—at all.

Flipping through the cable channels one evening, I stopped to listen to a TV preacher talk about salvation and getting right with God. Up to that point in my life, I hadn't had much to do with religion. While I was growing up, my family had been tangentially involved in Christianity. Although my father never attended any church activities, my mother sometimes attended a local Protestant church, and I went to the Sunday school on those occasions. Those classes exposed me to some of the stories and values that form the basis of Christianity. But I never really understood the big deal about Jesus Christ. Mom and I found the church people to be nice, and she especially enjoyed the potluck meals and the special events, but we were never active in the church or in the pursuit of genuine faith.

That spiritual apathy was the norm for me until age fourteen, when the brother of one of my best friends led an impromptu Bible study. He talked about our sin problem and how Christ had died on the cross to save us from the punishment we deserved. I was aghast. As he painted the picture—God's sacrificial love delivered through the murder of Jesus, necessitated by my wayward behavior and corrupted mind—it was clear that I needed to do something about it.

After that meeting, I began to pray constantly for forgiveness. When I say constantly, I mean just that: I literally prayed two to three hundred times each day, asking God to forgive everything I was doing and everything I had previously done. I was a wreck over the fact that I was a habitual, lifelong sinner! I did not have a relationship with Christ, only a foreboding fear of wrongdoing and the inevitable eternal punishment if I didn't get it right.

The church my friend attended was highly legalistic, and every time we went, we were bombarded with an overwhelming parcel of rules and regulations we needed to satisfy. It was truly unbearable, but having been scared out of my wits by this church's convicting doctrines about the wrath of God and the wickedness of man, I felt there was no escape. I had no choice but to keep trying to do better and to continually beg for forgiveness. Religion became the heaviest burden I had yet encountered.

The appeal of that religious group was that it provided clear-cut parameters and some semblance of stability for a young boy raised in a very dysfunctional family. When my father died, I became the man of the house by default. It was no easy responsibility to bear, and the combined expectations of God and family soon became too much for me to handle. I was on the verge of cracking up. Religion was only adding to my guilt and shame. No matter how hard I tried, I always felt that it wasn't enough and that I was losing ground on God's scale of perfection.

Later, I was introduced to Young Life, a national

parachurch ministry that works with teenagers. This group had a more balanced theology and was the first to teach me about God's grace in response to my sinful ways. As reassuring as that approach was, it led to major confusion in my mind. Was He a God of perfection, holiness, and grand expectations, or was He a God of love, forgiveness, and grace? I wanted to believe the latter, but I was fearful that it might be the former.

By the time I was in my junior year of high school, I hit the wall. Having reached my breaking point and seeing no way to reconcile the competing points of view and excessive demands associated with faith in God, I felt I had to flee the whole thing. I knelt down and prayed to God, asking Him to forgive me (of course!) for having to leave religion altogether. I confessed that if I did not give it up I would surely lose my mind. I was absolutely stressed over the confusion and weight that religion had laid on me, so I followed my instinct, which was to apologize and run.

For the next thirteen years, God was not part of the equation. I sealed off that part of my life and focused on doing the best I could with whatever morals, values, and character attributes I had gleaned by that time.

Now listening to the television preacher on that lonely night in July of 1991, I vaguely recalled hearing an intriguing comment attributed to Blaise Pascal, something about how each of us had a God-shaped hole in our hearts that only He could fill. That made sense to me. I had tried everything—money, drugs, sex, alcohol, travel, clothing, political influence, cars, houses—and I was still empty inside. The void that characterized my life could only be filled by something huge—something superhuman, something supernatural, something beyond the limitations of everything I had tried.

So with nothing to lose and everything to gain, on July 11, 1991, I fell to my hands and knees and asked Jesus into my heart. Little did I know that an attorney would one day defend me in court by quoting Jesus: "What good will it be for a man if he gains the whole world, yet forfeits his soul? Or what can a man give in exchange for his soul?" (Matthew 16:26).

With little else to live for at that point—retail sales failed to get my juices flowing—I got pretty pumped about the Christian faith and began reading the Bible and memorizing Scripture verses like crazy. I've always had a good memory, and since Christians seemed to treasure Scripture memorization, this was an easy way for me to get in the game. Eventually I decided to commit much of the New Testament to memory. That was me, all right: driven and over the top.

In retrospect, it would have been more helpful if I had devoted my time to simply understanding what a relationship with Christ meant and how to nurture it. But somehow I completely missed the fact that Christianity is not something you do, it is about a relationship with God and who you become through that divine connection. I had no idea at the time that my biggest issue in life was the superficiality of my character—or that the only antidote for that disease was a full-on commitment to allowing God to transform that character. Instead, I did what I had always done best: analyze, understand,

and act. Deciding to become a Christian was simply a calculated, intellectual choice, and my bull-in-a-china-shop approach to Christianity was characteristic of me: understanding something without emotionally investing in it.

A short while after becoming a Christian, I found that I had some time on my hands while the lawyers battled over my fate. I thought it would be fun to work with young people who were seeking to develop their faith in Christ, so I started volunteering with the local Young Life program. I met some outstanding people who were committed to serving the teenagers in the program, but despite the upswing in my spiritual life, there was no getting away from the increasingly claustrophobic legal realities that confronted me. After a year and a half of expensive, embarrassing, and contentious legal defense, I could no longer ignore reality. I was convicted of felony grand theft embezzlement and sentenced to five years in prison.

I was in a state of disbelief. Up to this point, I had never even given much thought to the charges that had been brought against me. I figured my lawyers would work things out and come up with a way for me to get out of the situation. Even though I had become a Christian, I still had such a disconnect with reality that it had been easy to live in a state of denial, focusing only on the here and now.

For the first time in my life, I was forced to face the consequences of my actions. My crime was considered among the more serious offenses a person can commit, short of murder or rape. Besides a stiff prison term, I lost some of my rights as an American citizen. I would no longer be allowed to vote unless I received a full pardon from the governor. I would not be able to serve on a jury or purchase firearms.

I would also be faced with additional restrictions after I was paroled. For the three years of my parole, I would not be allowed to drink alcoholic beverages. I would be required to submit to antinarcotic testing at the will of my parole officer. I would not be allowed to work in real estate or in professions closely associated with my offense, such as financial services. There could be no outside contact with Tony, my former business partner who was convicted of the same crime. Every time I applied for a job, I would have to inform the potential employer of my transgression. And I would not be allowed to start my own business.

On top of that, I was liable for multiple fines, taxes, and other payments—one of the fines alone was $750,000. I also would need to have regular check-ins with my parole and probation officers, could not live more than fifty miles from their location, and could not leave the area without their approval.

But I'm getting ahead of the story. Before I could enjoy the relative freedom of parole, I had to complete my prison term. I didn't realize it at the time, but my life was about to change. Dramatically.

CHAPTER 2

I Am H64741

Once we officially surrendered to the state corrections system, Tony and I boarded the bus headed for a distribution facility where our paperwork would be processed and our final destination determined. Because we were convicted in northern California, we began our time in the "reception" block of San Quentin, a temporary stop while the administration figured out where to send us to serve the bulk of our sentence.

Reception is perhaps too generous a word for the experience. Our receiving line was made up of hard-nosed corrections officers (known to prisoners as COs) who barked orders at the sad sacks exiting the buses as if it were the first day of Marine boot camp. I looked around at the other newly minted inmates, feeling increasingly uncomfortable. This was not where I wanted to be, and from the looks of things, these were not the people I wanted to spend the next few years of my life hanging out with. This was a far cry from Sigma Nu at Vanderbilt University, and these guys didn't remind me much of my happy-go-lucky, prank-loving fraternity brothers.

We were sent to our cells, each of which contained a generic bunk bed and little else. The massive cell block housed hundreds of identical cells. We all wore the same orange jumpsuits, which identified us as temporary visitors at San Quentin and gave everyone an immediate understanding of where we could and could not go within the huge prison complex.

I hadn't even become acclimated to prison life yet, and already the walls were starting to close in around me. Perhaps the hardest thing for me to deal with was the act of having my identity stripped away. I had reveled in the image of boy wonder. I had embraced the nickname Mr. GQ. I had inhabited the title "king of the party animals." But to the California Department of Corrections I had a less glamorous, more functional handle: H64741. That was my assigned number.

The COs had no problem treating me like a number. As we awaited our post–San Quentin assignment, I knew that to the guards and other officers I was nothing more than another dead weight on society, another scumbag caught by the justice system, another piece of human trash in serious need of reform. A number inside a silly orange jumpsuit.

Bill Dallas, for all intents and purposes, was a dead man. On February 1, 1993, I became H64741.

III

I was still in a state of disbelief over the fact that I was now officially a convicted felon and would have to live with that the rest of my life, but at least I was certain I wouldn't be confined in a maximum-security center like San Quentin for long. These places were reserved for the really bad boys.

Mine was a white-collar crime, and though it was a serious offense, I was not physically dangerous. The probability of someone like me plotting and executing a prison escape was minimal. Convicts of my ilk wanted to get on with our lives and would not risk having extra time added to the sentence because of an attempted escape.

During one of my first meals in San Quentin's chow hall, I stood in line and surveyed my dingy, damp surroundings. One line was reserved for temporary inmates like Tony and me. The permanent "mainline" prisoners entered through a different door. Dressed in their denim blue uniforms, these guys looked so hard and angry that I quickly breathed a silent prayer of thanks, relieved that I would be leaving San Quentin soon and never coming back to this dark place.

After two months in the reception area, Tony and I were sent to Susanville, a large prison complex in the California desert that had both a maximum-security and a minimum-security area. We were there to get a couple of months of firefighting training so that we could then be sent to a fire camp to complete our sentences. We were counting on doing our time at a place like Fairfield, a relatively relaxed fire camp in northern California where we would fight forest fires and clear combustible brush from the countless dry hills of that area. Every day we learned and practiced firefighting techniques and became competent at these tasks. It was good exercise, and the need to stay focused helped ward off the mental and physical anxiety of incarceration.

While we finished our training regimen, we lived in the minimum-security section of the complex, which was located just a few hundred yards outside the imposing walls of the maximum-security prison. Every day we would look at those massive concrete and steel walls, thankful that we were on the right side of them. Meanwhile, we waited expectantly for Fridays—the day when the new list of fire camp and prison transfers was posted.

I was particularly eager to get to Fairfield because that was much closer to where my parents and girlfriend lived. During my heyday, when money was flowing freely and the future looked as bright as the sun, I had moved my mom and step-father from Pennsylvania to northern California so they could be near me. Subconsciously, I think my desire to have them close may have been an attempt to show off just how talented and successful I was.

My upbringing had been neither normal nor especially healthy. My mother had given birth to my brother when she was just seventeen and still living at home. That was back in the 1940s, when such behavior was scandalous and brought serious disgrace to a family's image. Her family circulated in the well-to-do circles, so this pregnancy was a serious blow to the family reputation. The episode was such an embarrassment to my prim and proper grandmother that she put my mother on a train to California, where my brother was born. When my mother returned home, my grandmother made her continue to wear her maternity clothes, perhaps as a constant reminder of her sin and how she had besmirched the family name.

Somewhere in this whole mess my grandfather had taken to sexually molesting my mother, though this, too, was hidden from public view and never dealt with.

As a result, my mother had all kinds of physical and emotional struggles. She was also bipolar, so her mood swings were extreme and unpredictable, and she fought alcoholism for years.

Although my mother was devastated by my felony conviction and imprisonment, she and my girlfriend visited me regularly. It was a strain on all of us, but they were my main connection to the outside world, a link I desperately needed to retain any sense of hope for the future. Once in Fairfield, I knew I would be able to see them more often and stay connected to reality—the free-world reality.

So Tony and I held our breath every Friday when the new transfer list came down. Guys were assigned to fire camps all across California, and they were always so relieved to be placed in one of these camps.

At last, the day came when Tony's number was posted and he was assigned to a fire camp. We searched the list for my number, but it wasn't there. I rushed the CO and informed him they had made a mistake; my number was not on the list. He couldn't have cared less.

During the next few days, as Tony prepared to depart for his camp, I badgered the COs at every opportunity, imploring them to correct the mistake that obviously had been made. There was no doubt in my mind that the system had broken down and failed me—again.

Finally, my Friday arrived two weeks later. To my relief, my number was posted with a transfer to Fairfield on Tuesday of the following week! In just a few days I would be out of the desert and completing my time near my parents' home.

After what seemed like an eternity, Tuesday finally arrived. I was summoned by one of the guards, who took me to an administrative office. Just as we got inside the room, he turned to me and quietly said, "Trust me, God has a plan for you in all of this." I had no idea what he was talking about, though I didn't have much time to ponder his comment. Almost immediately, two other guards entered, handcuffed me, and walked me back to my bunk so I could clear out my locker.

"You're not going to fire camp," one of them said. "You're going back to maximum security."

What? I couldn't believe what I was hearing. Before I knew what was happening, they put me into a car and drove toward the maximum-security side of the prison. As we drove from one side of the prison to the other, I simply stared straight ahead, still in disbelief over the turn of events. Surely there had been a mistake.

Finally they dumped me out of the car. As I walked the pathway to my new cell in the maximum-security side of Susanville, carrying my belongings, I felt like a dead man walking. I was absolutely sure I would not survive if I had to stay in maximum security.

After a difficult and frustrating interrogation, I discovered that I had been rerouted from Fairfield and bumped to maximum security because prison officials thought I had been planning to escape! It turned out that after one of our visits, my girlfriend had driven past the fire camp at Fairfield to see where it was and what it looked like. Unfamiliar with the area, she pulled into one of its driveways and got too close to one of the restricted areas. She immediately realized that she had gone too far and became frightened, so she pulled a U-turn and sped away. As she did so, her elbow mistakenly hit the horn. The prison guards, ever watchful and sensitive to unusual behavior, traced the license plate number of her car. That led them to discover that she was listed in the database as a frequent visitor of a prisoner who was about to be assigned to the camp. They concluded that she must have been rehearsing an escape plan I had worked out with her. That made me, H64741, a flight risk, which also disqualified me from assignment to a minimum-security facility.

Although I tried to convince the officers that I hadn't even known about her visit to Fairfield, I knew it was pointless to try to argue my case. Discouraged and depressed, I was pretty sure things couldn't get much worse at that point. But I was wrong.

You cannot begin to imagine the rush of emotions that flooded my system when, after spending a couple of months at Susanville, I was given my transfer: I would be serving the remainder of my time in San Quentin.

If an alien ship from outer space had swooped down and whooshed me to the planet Xenon, I could not have been more stunned. How could a mistake of such colossal proportions have been made? Forget this H64741 stuff. I was Bill Dallas,

19

white-collar criminal, and I deserved to be on the next bus out, headed toward a minimum-security fire camp.

San Quentin? No way!

But there was no mistake. A couple of days after receiving my transfer, I found myself shackled into a narrow seat on a stuffy bus, riding with a group of inmates who were also being transferred to the least desirable of all state prisons. My wrists, ankles, and arms were all tightly cuffed by chains to a reinforced belt that encircled my waist. A guard with a shotgun aimed in our direction was stationed in a special compartment at the back of the bus.

I would soon be entering the house of terror known as San Quentin.

III

With twenty-twenty hindsight, I can now look back at the whole situation and realize that this was not merely God's plan for me: this was God's *best* plan for me because He loved me so much. My character was such a mess that it required a complete makeover. If I had joined Tony at a fire camp, such a retooling might never have happened. I would simply have served my time and emerged not much better off for the experience.

I would not have returned to a life of crafty deal making and high living, but neither would I have had a clue about how to put the pieces of my shattered life back together.

Just as He had done when He saved me from eternal

condemnation, God was now saving me from myself. This time, He was determined to build me up to be the man that He foresaw when I was just an embryo in my mother's womb. For more than three decades I had tried to mature via my rules, my way. Now it was time to grow His way.

God says He has a plan to give us a wonderful, hope-filled future (Jeremiah 29:11), and I can attest to the truth of that promise. I would rather have died than gone to San Quentin, but looking back, I recognize now that it was the only way God could have broken the pattern of selfishness that had become my way of life. I may have asked Christ into my heart, but He was certainly not deeply entrenched at the center of my life. I had faith, but it was not integrated into the fabric of my being.

I needed to be broken. And San Quentin was just the place to do it.

In the words of theologian A. W. Tozer, "It is doubtful whether God can use a man greatly until He has hurt him deeply."[1] I was about to become living proof of the truth of that statement.

CHAPTER 3

Embrace Your Trials

As our bus entered the exterior gate and then moved inside the walls of San Quentin, I found I couldn't take my eyes off the windowless, seventy-foot-high, yard-thick, steel and concrete walls. They seemed to have been built to convey a single message to prisoners: you are not getting out of here. And as I got off the bus, shackled and helpless, the truth of that message really hit home.

Once we arrived, things started to happen very quickly. This time around at San Quentin was different. First I was given my new wardrobe, and let's just say it fell a bit shy of my Armani taste. Everything was blue: denim shirt, denim jacket, and denim jeans. My boxers—and by the way, I had always worn briefs, a distinction that did not seem to matter to the guards—socks, and undershirt were white. No alligator belts. No Italian shoes. No variety. In fact, as I looked around the yard, I noticed that everyone was wearing the same ensemble.

The sameness, of course, was by design. It was not just for purposes of quick recognition: inmates in blue, COs in green, civilian and volunteer workers in any colors other than blue or green. Nor was it simply a tactic to prevent gangs from flashing overt signs of their presence. The unrelenting sea of blue was intended to send another message: you are not special. It was part of the process used to erase our former identities so the prison officials could replace them with ones more suitable to societal norms.

As we were marched through the facility toward our houses—that's what inmates called their cells—I noted another significant change: we couldn't get more than fifty yards or so without having to pass through a secure checkpoint. The complex was heavily populated with guards who sat at their assigned posts and checked the ID card of every person in their midst.

We had all been issued ID cards, and we were told that for all intents and purposes, they would be our keys to life. We couldn't leave our cells without them. We couldn't enter or exit the chow hall without them. We would not be allowed to go to our jobs inside the prison walls without them. Yet again San Quentin was sending me a message: You have no right to go where you want, when you want, for any reason you want. You forfeited that privilege when you exploited society. Your agenda is no longer up to you.

The guards explained that the ID cards were different colors, depending on the prisoner's status. A green card was issued to new guys and guys in reception—the area where I

had initially stayed while awaiting my not-to-be transfer to
Fairfield. Green cards gave prisoners no leeway whatsoever
because they were either temporary visitors waiting to be
reassigned or new inmates. A red card allowed its owner to
enter specified, restricted areas so he could perform his job.
The blue card was the most coveted, enabling prisoners to
move freely throughout the prison because the duties of their
jobs demanded such access.

I was given a green card, which meant I was low man on
the food chain. Until I earned greater privileges, that ID card
was my ticket to a very restricted territory. True to form, I was
disappointed with my picture on the card.

As we made our way to the cell that would be my new
home, I noticed the lines and signs on the ground. Many of the
signs were nearly impossible to read because they had been
worn down by voluminous foot traffic, but after studying them
for a while, I realized that they said "out of bounds." As I would
soon come to learn, prison officials were adept at reminding
us when we were out of bounds. These signs conveyed still
another message to me: know your place. I was no longer king
of my world; I was now subject to rules that had been made by
others and were enforced with daunting consistency.

We entered the North Block, one of the five huge wings
that housed the five thousand–plus inmates. As we slipped
through the entryway into the inner sanctum, the scene was
all too reminiscent of the prison movies I had seen prior to
my current ordeal: *Brubaker*, *An Innocent Man*, and others. I
looked up and saw five tiers of cells running the length of the

block. Each tier was exactly the same: fifty cells, side by side, lining the long corridor.

Directly across from the bank of cells was a catwalk, complete with armed guards. They patrolled with a deliberate gait, back and forth, eyeing the goings-on within the cells that stood perhaps twenty feet away.

Coming from the real estate market, I knew that location was everything. But in here I had no say in where I was placed. One of the COs started calling out our assigned cells. Mine was 4-N-10—fourth level, North Block, cell 10. It took me a moment to realize that there were no elevators in this place; every time I wanted to come in or go out, I would have to traipse up or down several sets of metal staircases.

We hoofed it up the stairs, the CO leading me to the fourth level where a guard was posted at the end of the floor. We walked down the narrow passageway as indistinct sounds echoed in the chasm between us and the wall next to the catwalk. I was starting to feel closed in. Even though I had known for a while that this day was coming, I wasn't ready for this moment.

The cell looked like a cramped closet. It was identical to every other cell in the building but seemed insanely miniscule, unfit for human habitation. Four feet wide, ten feet long. And *two* people were expected to live in that coffin.

A metal-frame bunk bed consumed most of the space. Beyond the bed was a cold steel toilet protruding from the back wall, with a steel sink bolted to the wall next to it. Weak light emanated from a couple of bulbs embedded in the wall.

The walls were hard cement. The floor was painted concrete. There were a few items on the floor, which I assumed belonged to my cellmate, who was lying on his mattress. It didn't dawn on me until later that these quarters were so tight that if he had been standing, he would have had to jump on the bunk to allow me to pass through to the rear of the cell. It's a dance that inmates quickly perfect.

I gawked at the rent-free residence California was providing me for the next few years. I didn't think there was any way that I could make myself walk into that tiny space. I had no history of claustrophobia, but standing there outside my cell door—my new home—I had the makings of a panic attack. For a few seconds that seemed liked an eternity I stared into the dimly lit, bland cell. As other newcomers on the same tier entered their new homes, I broke out in a cold sweat, paralyzed. The guard at the end of the hall yelled at me to get inside. Somehow, I don't know how, I managed to shuffle my feet twice and there I was, inside this cement box with metal bars. Behind me the cell door clanked shut.

And that was it. I was now in my new home, 4-N-10. I don't know how long I stood there with my eyes closed, willing the fear and anxiety to subside. During those interminable moments I prayed, silently crying out that this was more than I could bear. Where *was* He? Little did I know that God was indeed there, that He was helping me, that He knew I *could* bear it, and that this was all part of His perfect plan for my life.

Eventually my emotions calmed, and I looked around my new abode. It didn't take me long to get acquainted with the place.

III

Although I was not yet ready to acknowledge it, being sent to San Quentin was no accident. It was God's best plan for my life. My girlfriend's clumsy driving maneuvers at Fairfield were no accident; those "mistakes" were instrumental in me being sent where I needed to go. It was a God-orchestrated way for me to discover the power of accepting responsibility for my actions and the impact of relentless commitment to getting it right.

It would be years before the lessons of San Quentin would truly penetrate my being, but God knew this. And He was willing to wait.

Like those of us struggling with our demons in San Quentin, Nelson Mandela matured once he embraced the truth and value of his life's tribulations. Thanks to his trials, he blossomed into a great man who changed a country and maybe the world. Once a militant leader challenging the apartheid government in South Africa, Nelson Mandela was locked up on a remote island prison to blunt the effect of his strident attacks on the government and his stirring appeals for mass rebellion. By all accounts he was an intense but angry man. Blinded by that anger, he could not see that it merely diminished his influence and stole his freedom.

But twenty-seven years after he was first imprisoned, Mandela exited prison with a completely different demeanor— and impact. He had transitioned from a hostile combatant to a champion of reconciliation. His transformation so overwhelmed the people of South Africa that he became the first democratically elected black president of the nation.

I don't know what trials you are facing today, but I pray that you will consider how they might fit into God's *best* plan for your life. Though it was tough for me at first, the following principles helped me embrace my trials:

Learn from your troubles. Whatever your struggles are in life, don't focus on whether or not you consider them fair and just. Don't worry about whether other people have it easier than you or why some bad people seem to get away with more than you. Look your own troubles square in the eye, grasp the gravity and challenges of the situation, and learn everything you can from it. Those circumstances did not occur by accident. And if you ask God to give you the strength and wisdom to overcome and rise above those conditions and limitations, there is nothing you cannot accomplish. Believe me, I've seen it happen firsthand both in my life and in the lives of others.

A few years ago I heard author Chip Ingram speak about how to best perceive such conditions: "Our limitations are not prohibiters to God using our lives, but the very platform on which He chooses to display His grace."

Trust in the lordship of Christ. I came to San Quentin a weak man because my focus was on the things that stood in the way of my being who I thought I should be. Although I had asked Jesus Christ to be my Savior, I had not fully given Him the lordship of my life. Asking to be saved is a no-brainer; surrendering control of your life to someone else and allowing that person to call the shots is a whole different story. Making

Him my Lord meant giving up control and willingly going on the journey He orchestrated.

But I would soon learn that this was the first step toward becoming the man that God wanted me to be. Accepting the fact that we are all sinners and fall short of God's glory was difficult to internalize (Romans 3:23). And then being willing to admit and own my frailties and allow God to lead me down a very challenging path toward maturity were two other big steps. That's what Jesus had in mind when He told His disciples, "If anyone would come after me, he must deny himself and take up his cross and follow me" (Matthew 16:24).

Accept reality. Don't put another ounce of energy into making excuses or denying reality. Wholeheartedly embrace your troubles and invest yourself in overcoming and rising above them. Until you do so, your troubles own you. But once you accept them as stepping-stones to the great plans for which God has created you, your troubles cannot defeat you. They can only make you stronger and wiser for the challenges to come. In the words of Chuck Swindoll, "We are all faced with a series of great opportunities, brilliantly disguised as impossible situations." With the help of God, we can turn those impossible situations into stepping-stones to greatness.

TRANSFORMING PRINCIPLE

Your current troubles, trials, and tragedies just might be part of God's very best plan for your life.

CHAPTER 4

Cling to Hope—Even When You Can't See It

Once prison became my official residence, what began as fear quickly transitioned into dissolution and hopelessness.

My days began at 5 a.m. when our cell door was manually unlocked by a guard. We still couldn't get out because a second lock—a heavy steel crossbar—ran the entire length of the cell block, and it remained snug against the doors. The crossbar was not released until it was time for us to leave for breakfast around 7 a.m. To make sure we were ready, the COs used the loudspeakers to announce, "Chow in fifteen minutes." In the days before I entered prison, it would have taken me fifteen minutes just to get my hair looking right. In prison, I quickly learned that no one cared how I looked. Fifteen minutes was plenty of time to brush my teeth and throw on my clothes.

At first, it bothered me to get dressed without showering in the morning. In my prior incarnation as Mr. GQ, I had taken great pride in always being clean. But my enthusiasm for showers instantly evaporated when I took my first San Quentin shower: two hundred men sharing twenty shower-heads with only a few minutes to finish created an uncomfortable experience, to say the least. Whoever said "cleanliness is next to godliness" had obviously never taken a shower in a maximum-security prison.

We ate two meals a day in the chow hall: breakfast and dinner. The meals were mediocre, even for someone whose palate wasn't as refined as mine had been. Prison food consisted of anything that could be made en masse: mashed potatoes, rice, spaghetti, corn. Protein was supplied every day (eggs, peanut butter), and water was the primary drink. Coffee was always available, but it tasted more like faintly flavored water than a premium Starbucks blend.

It was standard practice for inmates to grab and consume food off the plates of those around them. That in itself took away my appetite for a while.

Lunch was delivered to us in a box, and we took it with us to our destinations: a job, the yard, our cell, or wherever we planned to pass our time that day. The box normally contained a couple of slices of white bread, a mystery meat sealed in plastic, a cookie, chips, a piece of fruit, and some type of powdered juice we could mix with water.

It didn't take me long to realize that the only way I was going to survive would be by relying on care packages from family (which we could get only once every three months) or through supplementary food I could buy from the canteen once a month.

Of course, I didn't *have* to go to meals. I didn't *have* to do anything in prison—except follow the rules. I didn't have to shower. I didn't have to go to the recreation area. I didn't have to exercise. I didn't have to get a job. But most inmates did those things because it gave them something to do and kept their minds off their situations. Passing time in prison was no simple task.

Some inmates chose not to work, so they spent their entire day hanging out in the yard. All kinds of things happened in the yard—chess and card games, ball games, exercise and weight lifting, and conversation. A field was also set aside for group sports like softball and soccer. We knew our afternoon free time was at an end when the loudspeaker cranked out, "Count time."

Part of the prison regimen was inmate counts. Everyone had to be accounted for at all times. Thrice daily we would have full-prison counts. During these exercises the red light on the security towers would be lit. Once the count was finished and everyone had been accounted for, the lights would be turned off. The process unfolded every day around 4 p.m., 10 p.m., and 3 a.m.

If anything was amiss, we'd go on lockdown and the prison would be shut up tighter than a drum. Sometimes we had to spend twenty-three out of every twenty-four hours in our cells during a lockdown. If we were allowed to go to the mess hall, it would be for a quick meal, no fooling around or dawdling. Other times, our meals would be brought to us and shoved through the cell doors by the guards. During these periods, every unnecessary thing was canceled: jobs, recreation, educational programs, visits, phone calls. Nobody liked lockdowns, which sometimes lasted two weeks or more. In a place of confinement, it was one of the most oppressive conditions, sharing our forty square feet with another man hour after hour after hour.

When we weren't on lockdown, we were allowed to participate in the programs offered after dinner until about 9 p.m. We could attend chapel, take educational classes (a lot of inmates were going for their GEDs), hang out in the yard, or participate in group meetings or practices (e.g., choir or band, AA sessions). By 9:30, everyone was due back in his cell.

For the first few months I was in San Quentin, I wasn't even able to see my family, since it takes visitors a while to go through all the necessary background checks for approval. Once they did, we met in a large room at the same time that other prisoners were meeting their guests. I spent most of our time together complaining about my situation, whining about my fate, and begging them to do whatever they could to get me reassigned.

I took very little pleasure in anything at that time, nor did I participate in any of the programs or activities offered to me. Even though I didn't have a job and did very little during the day, by evening I was usually ready to call it quits—not because I was looking forward to the next day, but because I was just plain exhausted. The hopelessness and humdrum of prison life wore me down. Besides, the sooner I got to sleep, the sooner the next day would arrive—and I would be one day closer to parole.

During my initial days at San Quentin, two thoughts monopolized my mind, swirling around in my head twenty-four hours a day:

Thought number 1: *It is not fair that I have to be in San Quentin.*

Thought number 2: *Nothing good can come out of this experience.*

There was no doubt in my mind that my presence with the rogues of this death trap was more than just a mistake; it was a tragedy of monumental proportions, and I alone was paying the price.

In my constant efforts to get out of San Quentin, I made life more uncomfortable for everyone than it already was. I pressured my sister into writing letters to congressmen, state officials, and prison officers to explain the details of my situation and enlist their assistance in transferring me to a more appropriate setting—one of the numerous fire camps for which I had been trained. I made a nuisance of myself to several San Quentin officials who, for some inexplicable reason, I believed could and would come to my rescue. My complaining got so bad that my cellie—the prison phrase for one's cellmate—told me to shut my mouth or he'd do the job for me.

Although I failed to act on it, one of the best pieces of advice I received in prison was offered by one of the friendlier guards. Watching me waste away day after day, he told me in no uncertain terms that there were only three things I needed to do every day: get out of bed in the morning, get dressed, and do something productive. In my state of total self-absorption and emotional paralysis, his words flew right past me. If confronted, I would have said that I was already doing those things. After all, they rousted us out of bed early each morning, whether we liked it or not. I showered regularly (well, maybe not regularly) and wore clothing, although I grew a beard that would have qualified me for a spot in ZZ Top. As for productive behaviors, eating and going to the bathroom seemed to fit the bill.

Before long, my hope for freedom, survival, and a meaningful life after prison faded, and one day I found myself curled up in the fetal position on the prison yard ground, moaning and sobbing. My deepest desire was simply to die. Life had gotten the best of me, and I was ready to roll over and give up. I had no apparent reason to continue now that justice had crushed me and my life was irreparably ruined.

I spent an entire month—a *month*—curled into that ball in the prison yard. Inmates passing by looked at me with disgust. I was not a man; I was just a pathetic, miserable, self-absorbed sack of flesh and bones. Finally one day, I seemed to hit rock bottom. As I whimpered to myself about the hopelessness of my circumstances, I felt completely buried by the intense, deep sense of despair that had washed over me. Helpless, I looked up and saw that the massive cement wall across the yard had disappeared and was replaced with utter darkness. I had never seen or imagined such a dense place, completely void of all light. The blackness was overwhelming. As awful as I had felt since arriving at San Quentin, this was a whole new level of despair. A feeling of absolute nothingness took over my being. I was scared and panicky—utterly alone.

I wondered what was happening to me. Something was sucking the life out of me. Was this hell on earth? I was beyond terrified. It was as if I had transcended fear of anything known or unknown, and what I found was that the only thing that lay beyond abject fear was complete hopelessness.

In that minute I understood why someone would commit suicide. I was at the edge of human reality and was barely clinging to that edge with my fingernails. Instinctively I knew things could not get worse than this. If there was anything worse than what I was feeling at that moment in my life, I knew I could not possibly bear it.

"Get up," someone said to me. It was more of an invitation than a command. I looked up at the voice, expecting to see a guard, but instead I saw it was just another inmate, someone I walked past every day. I closed my eyes to return to my torment, uninterested in whatever this guy was selling.

I had seen this inmate around, but we weren't exactly blood brothers. I had no idea what his name was or what cell block he came from. Was this a ploy to get me into an isolated corner where he and few inmates could beat the life out of me? Was this an initiation rite for some prison group? Was he about to make me an offer I couldn't refuse? Was it my turn to be his "girlfriend"?

"Come on, let's go," the voice continued. I was too depressed to care. He could lay his whole sales pitch on me, for

what—Islam, the North Block softball team, Tupperware—
I didn't care. I just wanted him to say his piece and move on.

But he didn't go away. In fact, he pulled me up off the
ground and helped me to stand. Then he started moving me
toward the old brick building to one side of the yard where the
old dungeons of San Quentin used to be.

"We're gonna get you a job," he said.

I had no idea what he was doing or why. Maybe he got a
commission for each lump of humanity he hustled into some
recruiting office. I was glad someone was aware of my existence, but couldn't he see that I was midstride in my daily pain
performance?

"You need to get your mind off your problems and on to
something productive," he explained as we moved toward the
dungeon. "You're not doing yourself any good just wasting
away on that dirt every day. A job will help you get through
this."

I don't know what was going through his head, but I
imagine he expected me to see the wisdom in his comments.
I didn't.

When we finally reached our destination, it turned out to
be the home of the prison's television station, SQTV. The station broadcast original and educational programming within
the compound several hours each day. I was only vaguely
aware of the existence of the station; it was irrelevant to my life
at that time.

We entered a small office that was inhabited by a guy
who turned out to be the station manager, an employee doing

a nine-to-five job inside the walls. My new friend briefly explained my situation and asked the manager to give me a job.

When the station manager said he wasn't sure if they had any openings at the moment, the inmate asked again, this time with more emphasis: "This guy *really* needs a job." The manager, whose name was Larry, sighed and simply said, "Okay, I'll find him something."

I was leaning against one of the walls, not really part of their exchange. I was more like a piece of extra furniture. Yet I did not feel uncomfortable in this place. It was probably the only building on the prison grounds that had no windows, and that was a good thing. Darkness matched my mood and had become a welcome friend for me; I disliked the light of day.

But this entire charade seemed absurd to me. I could not imagine what good a job would do for me. I was too depressed to contribute anything of value. If they'd had an opening for a zombie, well, I was their man, but that didn't seem too likely.

Larry made a quarter turn and looked me over. Thinking back on the scene, I'm amazed he didn't burst out laughing at the pathetic excuse for a human being that was leaning against the wall in his tiny office. My head was down, eyes closed, and my arms were wrapped tightly around my body. I had dirt all over my clothing and mud stains on my face from spending time on the ground crying.

My inmate friend thanked Larry, patted me on the back, and walked out. My internal fear meter raced to the top of the scale, wondering what would happen next.

Larry looked at me for a long moment, then smiled and

simply said, "Get that broom over there and sweep out the studio, okay?" Once the request registered in my brain, I shuffled into the adjoining large area, which apparently was one of their studios, and began absentmindedly sweeping nonexistent dirt.

I returned to SQTV every day for the duration of my time in San Quentin. During the first few months, I wound up doing menial tasks: sweeping, labeling tapes, filing, making coffee, and the like. To his credit, my fellow felon was correct: getting my mind off my own crisis and on to other things, no matter how trivial, seemed to begin to pull me out of my tailspin and get me on the path toward hope.

Although I didn't realize it at the time, this would be the start of my reentry to life.

III

Before prison, I was the epitome of confidence and hope. I did not have a real relationship with Jesus Christ during those years and felt no need for one. The world was ripe for the picking, and I was a John Deere harvester combing through the fields.

My hope was 100 percent in Bill Dallas. I had the abilities, a dream, and the drive to make that dream my reality. So what if my character was questionable? My life was moving a thousand miles a minute in the direction I wanted. My hope was in making the dream happen, and things were on track for my hope to be fulfilled.

All of that confidence fell apart the minute I walked through the gates of San Quentin. And when despair threatened to completely overwhelm me, I knew I had lost all control. That moment was devastating on multiple levels. The absence of light and the intense loneliness were crushing. Feeling trapped in a slice of time that knew no boundaries was excruciating. And being absolutely helpless to do anything about it was something I had never experienced before.

I knew I didn't have the strength to pull myself out of my despair. Are you kidding me? In those days I didn't have the strength to enter my cell without people shoving me in, so how was I going to resist the elimination of all hope?

I could relate to Job's ordeal. In defending his innocence he asked his friends, "Where then is my hope? Who can see any hope for me?" (Job 17:15). But I also believe that what I was feeling was similar to the sense of total abandonment and emptiness that Jesus Christ felt when He was betrayed and crucified, and died. Theologically speaking I know his experience was much more intense than mine. He took on all the sins of the world to save us from our own corruption, but I was shattered by my own small glimpse of what it must have felt like.

The irony of the fact that SQTV was located in the prison's old dungeon did not strike me until years later. I was a dead man entering the dungeon, but it was my time spent in that place of death that helped restore life and excitement to me. In the Bible, God used the desert, seas, mountains, and even battlefields as sites of restoration. And now He added the dungeon of San Quentin as yet another life-transformation location.

My path to hope was facilitated by a group of inmates

known as Lifers. These men had been sentenced to a life term, which usually lasted at least twenty years. Yet many of them seemed to take joy in helping others get their lives on track. When I was in my most desperate state, one of these inmates grabbed me and literally put me on my feet. But although he lifted me up, he wasn't willing to carry me. It wasn't until I actually started walking on my own that the other Lifers began to rally around me. It wasn't a big show of support or an organized expression of concern. A few of them simply began to notice and interact with me. I suspect that many of them had been through a similar bottoming-out moment and recognized the symptoms in me. They had mercy on me, and I was all too happy to accept their support.

Obviously, the way these inmates showed love was not by hugging me or telling me how great I was. They simply made me part of their circle and kept me in the loop—a question here, a comment there, a suggestion at a key moment. It was all very unspectacular, almost stealthy. The brief times of interaction with them seemed to come out of nowhere at first, but I eventually began to look forward to them. It was as if I was being accepted into the Lifers' family, but it had to be done slowly, one step at a time. And the cumulative effect was that these men gave me hope.

There wasn't any kind of overnight resurrection of Bill Dallas. I continued in my depression for quite some time. But without even realizing it, I began to draw strength from these men. Just being near them and seeing their self-assurance lifted my spirit. They had an air of confidence and peace that was appealing and reassuring.

For the remainder of my sentence I intentionally watched and analyzed them. I wanted to know what made them tick. I saw them through a different lens now, and I began to trust them.

The Lifers possessed a strong hope for their own lives. They walked the yard with a self-confidence based on the hope they had of being and becoming people of worth and purpose, no matter what their circumstances.

It was the short-timers—the ones like me who would soon be back on the streets, with their families, in their normal environment—who were the most hopeless. As a short-timer, I didn't see it that way, of course. But a major reason I lacked sustainable, genuine hope was that I was focusing on the negative aspects of life: the injustice of my imprisonment, the faults of others, the unfairness of the world, the disadvantages I suffered, and so on. I lacked uplifting, meaningful goals for life, and I stayed angry, focusing on the unfairness of my past and my need to control life.

Thank God the Lifers dragged me out of that short-timer state of mind. In retrospect, I see how their treatment of me was a flesh-and-bones representation of what Jesus has done for me. My connection with Him is deeper today than it has ever been—but it all started with Him loving me first.

During my stay in prison, the hope in my heart grew from a tiny seed to a vibrant vine blossoming with expectation. It grew slowly—it probably took a good six months for me to shed my depression and believe in myself and my future—but it happened! Before long, I was not just eager to get out from behind the walls of San Quentin, but also about starting over again and doing something special with my life. I had no idea what that would be. But when hope is restored, the details don't seem to get in the way.

That's one of the hallmarks of hope: it flows from the faith that *what you don't know cannot stop you from doing what you have never done.* Hope is not just a good feeling about what's to come. Hope is an improbable but unshakable certainty that things will work out.

Jeremiah hit the nail on the head when he told the Israelites, "Blessed is the man who trusts in the LORD, whose confidence is in him" (Jeremiah 17:7). When you hit rock bottom, you may finally realize that God is your only true hope. Even when all conditions point to doom, know that God never abandons those who love Him. Isaiah put it well when he foretold that in spite of their dire circumstances, the Israelites ultimately would be taken care of, noting that God provides for those who trust Him and keep their thoughts fixed on Him (Isaiah 26:3). That promise is still valid for you and me today.

Even though it was not clear to me at the time, prison was part of God's best plan for me—a plan that would reshape my character so that He could use me in the future for His purposes. How many of us experience strange or painful eras of life, confused as to why a holy, loving, and omnipotent God would allow one of His beloved children to undergo such difficulties? But if we truly believe that He loves us and that He is in control of our lives, and if we allow Him to have His way with us, we will emerge in a better place. Whether the burden we bear is a prison sentence, a debilitating disease, financial collapse, a dissolved marriage, or the death of a loved one, God has a plan to use that hardship for our good and the advancement of His Kingdom.

What can be done if you or someone you know loses hope? Here are some of the things that worked for me.

Change your environment. In my case, an inmate had to literally pull me up out of the dirt. It's hard to see past the things that have become familiar and comfortable. To shake up your head and heart you need a change of scenery: routine, location, relationships, job, goals—whatever it takes.

Force yourself to adopt a new perspective on life. It was hard to do, but watching the Lifers and imitating them made it possible for me to alter my thinking. Surround yourself with people whose points of view will challenge your thinking and move you forward. You need the stimulation of new ideas and divergent ways of thinking.

Hold on until hope returns. If you are serious about making a comeback, you have to stick with it until things start to turn around. God's track record is one of allowing His chosen people to endure hardships before He lifts them out of those circumstances. Perseverance is a required tool for fixing what's broken in your life. In a great sermon I heard once, the pastor said, "When you can't see His hand, trust His heart." You have to hold on until God is ready to change your situation; hope is knowing that because He loves you, He *will* come.

<table>
<tr><td>TRANSFORMING PRINCIPLE</td></tr>
<tr><td>*Even when it seems that hope is nowhere to be found, hold on and wait for its return.*</td></tr>
</table>

CHAPTER 5

Express Yourself through Your Work

Most inmates had prison jobs; they gave them something to do and took their minds off their situations. Jobs started after breakfast around 8 a.m. and wound up around 3 p.m. We received monetary credit in our commissary accounts—a few cents a day, plus one day taken off our sentences for each full day of work completed.

The inmates who had the shortest sentences got the worst jobs, tasks like cleaning the toilets, washing dishes in the chow hall, or sweeping the yard. Those jobs paid the least and were the most physically taxing and the least prestigious—although, come to think of it, there weren't many jobs in the system that smacked of status.

The primo jobs were held by the Lifers. These positions were usually indoors and administrative in nature. They were desirable because they allowed inmates to work with influential staff members and perhaps get some very minor benefits from that relationship. The perks were never anything illegal or extraordinary, just little things like the ability to request extra blankets, a specific book from the library, or an extra telephone call on occasion. The biggest advantage of these jobs was that they provided inmates with more respect and opportunities to travel more freely within the prison compound with the prestigious blue ID card.

An inmate with a good job had plenty of "juice"—prison-speak for clout. The more influential the boss, the more juice a prisoner had. Those who didn't have juice wanted to buddy up with someone who did. Inmates might be stripped of identity and possessions, but we all had an innate drive to figure out ways to work the system. Following the trail of influence was instinctual for most of us; it is what got some of us in trouble in the first place.

When I began working at SQTV, I was in survival mode—barely—and was simply doing what I was told. But as time progressed, I began to feel more alive because of that job. It wasn't because of the money; I was getting about thirty cents an hour. But the low pay produced another lesson: the job was so special because it restored my spirit and focused my mind, not because it inflated my spending account.

One of the reasons I had blasted out of the starting gates after college had been my desire to avoid the living hell that my father had experienced. He had grown up filled with promise and hope. He was a tennis champion and an Ivy League graduate, with high hopes for a great acting career. But his father strictly forbade him from pursuing such a frivolous profession, especially after completing a stellar education.

The result was that my father went into the same industry that his father did: insurance. He worked hard at it but hated every minute of it. Although selling corporate insurance policies was not his calling, he took his family responsibilities very seriously, providing a decent life for his wife and children while making his parents proud.

But it took a monstrous toll on him. The star athlete became an alcoholic who smoked two packs of cigarettes a day and was fifty pounds overweight. Every night he dragged himself through the front door after another mind-numbing day doing something he had no passion for, plopped himself in his favorite chair, and began his nightly anesthetizing process.

Sadly, my father died at the age of fifty-one. In reality, he had probably died twenty-five years earlier, but his body didn't realize it. He was, in effect, operating on emotional life support for a couple of decades.

There is nothing more frustrating than watching a talented person squander his life. It is all the more agonizing when that person is your father and you feel helpless to do anything about it.

I had been determined not to follow in his footsteps. There were too many exciting and inviting opportunities in the world to get stuck in a life-draining rut. I was fortunate to get into a top-rated school; I worked hard at my studies and looked forward to taking on the world—on my terms.

Sure enough, during my blitzkrieg years in real estate, I *did* have the time of my life, even though it was all an illicit facade undertaken at the expense of innocent people. It didn't matter to me as long as I remained true to my promise to go for what I wanted and pursue it with all of my energy.

As unethical as my behavior was, one of the most infectious outcomes of those years was the tremendous joy I received from setting my mind on a goal and throwing myself at it full bore. I took a great deal of pleasure in accomplishing challenging objectives and knowing that I had the talent and strength to make significant things happen.

But my experience in San Quentin taught me an equally important lesson: such joy and gusto can quickly be lost if it is based on nothing more valuable than outward success and financial power. My crash-and-burn act was imperative for the rebuilding of my character, but it left me in a state of befuddlement for a long time.

Before I started working at SQTV, I had no goals, no responsibilities, and no productive activities. The lack of focus and purpose turned me into a tragic figure. I lost all sense of myself because I did not have a mechanism for expressing my gifts and vision. Without meaningful work, I had no productive outlet for revealing and refining who I was. Without a job that extracted such value, I slowly lost my identity, purpose, voice, energy, and hope.

The need to do something truly productive—something that added value to lives other than my own—didn't hit home until I took the SQTV position. The SQTV experience sparked a miraculous turnaround in my life, eliciting a sense of purpose and productivity in me for the first time since being drummed out of the real estate development market. I learned everything I could about television production and eventually wound up running the cameras, designing the sets, directing programs, producing special events, and being the on-air talent in various shows.

One show I put together was a special called *The 100 All-Time Best Movies as Voted by the Inmates of San Quentin*. Clearly, program titling was not one of my strengths. The program itself, though, was enthusiastically received by the audience. The content was based on a survey I conducted among the inmates to generate the top 100 list. And the movie they rated as number one was *The Godfather*. Go figure!

Eventually, I worked my way up to producer and on-air talent of my very own show. Granted, it wasn't exactly HBO or ESPN—if everyone inside the complex had been tuned in to our station, my maximum audience was still only five thousand people—but my mind was being challenged with useful thoughts and my work made an impact on at least a few lives. Usually we profiled inmates, guards, and other prison workers, but once in a while, I was able to bring in some outside guests, including NFL great Ronnie Lott and comedian Paul Rodriguez. It was my own little Oprah show!

Inmates soon got used to me running up to them with a microphone and camera gear so that I could interview them about things happening in the prison or ask for their thoughts about prison life and various world events.

I was under no delusion that my closed-circuit TV shows

would change the world. But that job did change my own life, and I knew that those shows gave inmates a respite from the drudgery of prison life. We did some fun things, like the movie review program, that incorporated inmates as guests. They loved to ham it up and got a real kick out of seeing themselves and other inmates on air. For some, it was their proverbial fifteen minutes of fame; more often, though, it was fifteen minutes of innocent fun, a unique creative outlet for men who had few chances to be original.

I am pretty sure that few of the inmates realized that the energetic, upbeat guy asking the questions was the same bearded, broken guy who had spent so much time not too many months earlier groveling on the grass and crying. My work gave me a new lease on life. I took great pride in the work I produced, and it helped to restore my punctured self-image.

One of my favorite movie scenes is from the classic *Chariots of Fire*. In one segment, the champion Scottish runner Eric Liddell is being chastised by his ministry-minded family for running in races rather than going directly to the mission field. His response was profound: "I believe God made me for a purpose, but He also made me to run fast. And when I run, I feel His pleasure." I was quickly coming to understand what he meant.

III

We get joy and fulfillment from doing work because God made us to work. In his search for meaning in life, Solomon concluded that while the ultimate purpose of life is to love and obey God, working is one of the ways in which we obey Him and add value to His creation. In fact, when God created Adam, one of the first things He did was give him some work to accomplish: taking care of the Garden and animals. He created Eve as a helper for that responsibility. This all took place before their sin; work was a gift from God, not a curse.

The Bible provides a perspective on the role of work in our lives. Accepting the responsibilities that come with a job gives us an opportunity to serve God and other people, provides a means for satisfying our material needs and those of our families, gives us an outlet for the abilities and skills God has given us, and even provides resources that we can use to bless others who are less fortunate or have a specific need (see Ephesians 4:28; 2 Thessalonians 3:10; 1 Timothy 5:8).

Paul reminds us that our performance at work is part of God's grand plan for humanity: "We are God's workmanship, created in Christ Jesus to do good works, which God prepared in advance for us to do" (Ephesians 2:10).

When we find the sweet spot of our interests, abilities, and God-given opportunities, our work—and lives—becomes a joy for us and, in all likelihood, for God. It's not always easy to find that sweet spot, but the following steps might be helpful.

Do what you love. My father gave up doing the things he was most drawn to because he thought it was the responsible thing to do. But when we turn our backs on our God-given abilities and talents, we're also giving up the opportunity to spend our lives doing what we love. God gave me a head for business and marketing, and when I use my skills for His glory rather than my own gain, the joy and satisfaction that follow are beyond description.

My job at SQTV was significant because it gave me something to focus upon, a reason to get up every morning, and an outlet for my creativity. It had nothing to do with money or fame or power.

Understand that God is pleased when you do what He made you to do. When I was in prison, I heard a radio teacher say that we glorify God most completely when we live most fully as the human beings He designed us to be. We are given all kinds of resources with which to serve Him: natural skills and abilities, spiritual (supernatural) abilities, relationships, ideas, intelligence, experiences, opportunities, and other resources. The combination of those elements gives us a chance to express ourselves and experience the fullness of this life. Rick Warren stated it this way: "Work becomes worship when you dedicate it to God and perform it with an awareness of his presence."[2]

On balance, then, it seems that Solomon was right about the value of work in our lives. Over the years since leaving San Quentin, I've experienced ups and downs in my career, but the more committed I am to owning my job and producing something that I can proudly offer as a gift to God—no matter what the nature of the job is—the more satisfying that work becomes. There are times when obstacles and difficulties make me want to quit, but remembering that work is a gift from God that enables me to honor Him and develop my character keeps me going. After all, it's not "just a job." Our work is a way for us to become the servants that God formed us to become, a way for us to fulfill our roles in the grand plan He has for humanity while reaping the benefit of obeying Him and blessing others. That, in itself, is an incredible gift from God.

TRANSFORMING PRINCIPLE

God wants you to express yourself through meaningful work.

CHAPTER 6

Choose Sustaining Faith

Although I had asked Christ to be my Lord and Savior shortly before my conviction, my faith seemed to wither once I entered prison. At that point, survival became my highest priority. Yes, I had really wanted to develop a deeper and more meaningful relationship with God. But that desire had not yet been translated into a lifestyle that made my faith real—not because I refused to do so but because I didn't know how.

The plan of activity I had devised after I accepted Christ included memorizing hundreds of verses, studying for hours on end, praying, listening to sermons, and much more. It was enough to give even the most driven person a panic attack! Those kinds of tasks were all well and good, but I was clearly missing the point of what it meant to have a relationship with God. He wasn't looking for a spiritual laborer, He was seeking a companion. Unfortunately, I had so completely filled my schedule with spiritual tasks, there was no time left just to be with Him.

My goal was to make God proud of my hard work on His behalf, but I didn't realize that God was less interested in what I did than in who I was. With the harried agenda of spiritual effort to which I had committed myself, I never got the chance to experience real intimacy with Him. My flurry of activity actually produced the exact opposite outcome of that which I so passionately desired.

And as a result, my faith was simply not strong enough to sustain me during those initially dark days behind the walls of San Quentin.

I first met Vy Le when he was working in the chapel at San Quentin. A small-framed man from Vietnam, Vy was always smiling—a rarity in a maximum-security prison. He moved about with an air of self-confidence, peace, and joy. He reminded me a bit of Mr. Miyagi, the karate instructor in the *Karate Kid* movies, but he was much younger.

At that time, I was still deep in the throes of depression, and I often tried to slink into the back of the chapel where I could just be alone for long stretches of time. I always sat in the back corner, trying to hide in the shadows, though I'm sure Vy couldn't help but notice me since I was the only one in the room sobbing uncontrollably.

Finally one day, Vy came over and sat down. He didn't say anything at all. He just sat next to me, letting me know that he was there and that he cared.

Over the following weeks and months as I slowly began to emerge from the mental and emotional fog that had enveloped me, I realized that although Vy hadn't really done anything special, his presence alone had given me strength. He did not say the right words or do anything particularly impressive. He just offered me security and shelter from a confusing world by his willingness to sit with me.

I coveted the peace and understanding that Vy and other Lifers like him seemed to have. Most were devoted Christians, but theirs was not just a "head faith"—all information and no action—these guys really got it. They had what I was searching for—and I wanted to know how to get it too.

A few of the Lifers were clearly predators, the worst of the worst—so deeply and completely corrupted that only a phenomenal work of God could place them on the path to recovery. But they were the exception to the rule. To my surprise, most of the Lifers had been transformed. They hadn't always been that way, of course. The majority of them had committed awful crimes: murder, armed robbery, rape, kidnapping. But somewhere along the way, they simply reached the end of themselves, coming to the realization that they were powerless to rise above their circumstances without divine intervention. Once this realization became clear, their lives were never the same again.

I began hanging out with the Lifers as often as I could, eager to pick up pointers about their faith and coping skills. They became the first genuine community of faith I had ever experienced. These guys had a spiritual humility I had never witnessed before. They truly cared about me.

If they asked how I was doing, they stopped to listen to my answer because they really wanted to know. They did not recite memorized prayers but instead talked to God with sincerity and conviction. They discussed their struggles to apply biblical principles in vulnerable, honest ways. There was no pretense. They were unconditionally accepting of me and others.

San Quentin dislodged my perception of the church as an institution and redefined it as a unified group of sinners who were so thrilled to be accepted by God that they accepted everyone who wanted to join them on the journey. Their emphasis was love, not rules; character, not attendance; spiritual fruit, not information retention.

I had belonged to churches before entering prison and had even been in classes and small groups where people got to know each other pretty well. But growing up in a dysfunctional family, I had never really known what it was like to draw strength from the presence of others.

Frankly, one of the reasons I had never been a die-hard church person was that I felt I could never meet the standards that had been set. Despite all the talk about accepting people as they were, the churches I had attended had expectations that had to be met before you were fully accepted. These included things like the quality of your clothing, your public piety, your ability to speak the lingo, the behavior of your children, your knowledge of basic Bible verses, and your willingness to speak publicly and articulately about your faith.

But at San Quentin, I finally found a church that was willing to take me in regardless of my lack of qualifications. It was the first time I had ever met people who practiced Jesus' command not to judge unless you want to be judged.

The Lifers were genuinely happy when I was with them, no matter what my crimes and idiosyncrasies were. It was the first time I had been with a group of Christians who had memorized fewer Scripture passages than I had. But none of them cared about that. They loved me no matter how much or how little I knew. It was my initial experience with a body of believers who believed that the Bible is completely true but still acknowledged that we would probably misinterpret the Scriptures on occasion.

As I watched the Lifers, I was reminded of a conversation I had with Harvey Morgan before my conviction. A member of the Virginia House of Delegates, Harvey was the father of a good friend of mine and a man of great faith and character. I had shared with him my struggle to know God more intimately and to overcome the feeling that I was never "good enough" in my faith. Harvey explained that God loved me completely; He could not love me any more than He already did, and I just needed to relax and let His love come to me. At that point, I had a tough time incorporating this message of grace into my way of thinking, but in San Quentin, I could see the concept lived out on a daily basis.

One of the most important things I noticed about the Lifers I looked up to was that, to a man, they had all given control of their lives to Christ. This, to me, was quite a remarkable feat. Here was a group of men who, for the most part, were serving life sentences precisely because they had refused to surrender control to anyone and had stubbornly followed only their own rules and choices. These were highly self-reliant people. I could definitely relate to this character flaw; my own downfall had been facilitated by my refusal to let others have a say in how I conducted my business affairs and carried out my leisure life.

But even though this was one of the most spiritually, racially, and socioeconomically diverse groups I had ever encountered, the men all had one radical commonality: each of them had handed the reins of his life to God. Although they had traversed different paths in their journey with God, they had all relinquished the leadership of their lives to the only one who could perfectly guide them forward. For many of them, giving up control had been a struggle. For every one of them, it was a transforming choice.

I also realized that these men followed personal disciplines in order to maintain their connection to God. So I began to do the same. I woke at 5 a.m. each day just as the prison was coming to life and spent time reading my Bible, drinking my coffee (instant Folgers mixed with the hottest water I could get from my sink), and just meditating on God. Having been more of a night animal during my real estate days, rising before the sun came up was a new experience for me. But oddly enough, this became my most cherished time of day. I loved the opportunity to read, pray, listen, and meditate, and I looked forward to it. On days when something disrupted that schedule, I felt cheated.

III

The true church is a community that shares intimacy with each other and with God, and that radiates the hope that

Christ places in our hearts. San Quentin taught me that I am not so much called to *go* to church as I am to *be* a living representation of the church—the body of Christ. It is likely that I will never again find exactly the same kind of community I had with the Lifers. But I can help build a different but equally valid and valuable community of faith.

We have been fully forgiven and are fully loved, and we have no reason to feel guilty or unworthy when we're with the Lord. That's the gift that Jesus' resurrection bought for us. If you are looking for the secret to spiritual vitality, consider the following things I observed in the Lifers.

Surrender control of your life to God. It's not easy for Americans to give up control of our destinies. We admire those who keep control over their lives and make something of them. We teach young people the skills required to maintain their independence. Even our national ethos is based on the idea that nobody will tell America what to do or force its will upon this country.

Who controls your life? That is a question you ought to really think about. The knee-jerk response of most Christians is to claim that God is in control, but I suspect we overestimate how much authority we knowingly and freely grant Him in our lives. And I'm pretty sure we underestimate the toll it takes on us when we don't give Him total dominion in our lives. In my observation, this is one of the biggest challenges facing the church in America. We allow Him to be our Savior, but we do not really allow Him to be the Lord of our lives. How are you doing in that regard?

Commit to having a vibrant relationship with God.
Christians talk about fellowship with God a lot, but surveys
suggest that surprisingly few believers have a dynamic friendship with Him.[3] The experience of the Christians in Ephesus
reminds us that it is also possible to start out full of passion
and zeal for God, but to burn out along the way, losing that fire
in the belly for Christ (Revelation 2:4). It is a danger to which
all believers are susceptible.

Every solid relationship takes serious effort. Wanting it is
not enough. You have to aggressively pursue that friendship.
Jesus didn't die to advance religion; He gave Himself up so that
He could have a relationship with us. But that interaction is
never automatic. As in any good friendship, you have to probe
it, experiment with it, and invest in it. What kind of investment
are you making in your relationship with Jesus these days?

Relax in your faith. American culture is founded on the
notion of accomplishing specific outcomes. Our heroes are
people who did outstanding things. The companies we revere
are those that shatter performance and productivity standards.
We want to see the track record.

But heaven's culture is based on luxuriating in the presence
and majesty of God. When you are with your best friend, you
are able to forget your cares and relax. And that's how it should
be in our relationship with God. As Brennan Manning says,
"God loves you as you are and not as you should be."

This doesn't mean that we ought to become complacent
or wimpy, but that we should pursue a faith that is tranquil
and not burdensome. This is a real challenge for American

Christians. Inmates describe people as "stressing" when they aren't able to let go of a situation and let life flow. The same principle holds true in the faith realm: it's often hard for us to abandon our guilt, embrace grace, appreciate the pain involved in real growth, and simply enjoy the presence and working of God in our lives.

We often stress over our faith, as if we are not doing enough to please God. We forget that Jesus said, "Come to me, all you who are weary and burdened, and I will give you rest. Take my yoke upon you and learn from me, for I am gentle and humble in heart, and you will find rest for your souls. For my yoke is easy and my burden is light" (Matthew 11:28-30). How consistently and completely are you able to relax with God?

Participate in a community of faith. The Christian life is much easier when you pursue it in the company of like-minded people. This is a critical element of being part of the church and becoming spiritually healthy. But it is not as easy as it sounds.

First, you have to dedicate yourself to the community; being in relationship with others is a conscious choice and takes consistent effort. Belonging and participating are two different things. You can belong to an organization, in the sense of being an accepted member, without being invested in the life of that group. In order for it to be a community, there must be the sharing of life. Such intimacy does not happen without a commitment of identity, time, and energy. And that commitment encompasses a willingness to engage in activities that might be outside your comfort zone or range of interests. (The early church described in Acts 2–7 is a great example of the ends to which members go to be an organic part of the community.)

Second, you have to be willing to be vulnerable. If you do not trust the people in the community, you cannot expect the connection to go deep. Vulnerability includes, but is not limited to, transparency. It includes freely giving love, respect, and value to those in the group.

Third, attitude goes a long way toward determining if your connection with a community will be sustainable. That means allowing yourself to experience joy from being with these people and excitement over the things God is doing in their lives.

There's even an unsophisticated but effective test to discern whether or not you are truly part of a community. Consider how often you look for opportunities to bring new people into your circle of friends. The more open and assertive you are in doing so, the more meaningful that community is to your life.

Are you a participant in a genuine community of faith, or have you settled for religious routine? As you evaluate how you fit within the community of faith, what kind of expectations and example do you bring to the party? Christ has begun to do great things within you and through you, and He will continue to refine you until He returns (Philippians 1:6). Let Him finish the job, and then share that growth with others!

TRANSFORMING PRINCIPLE

God wants us to have sustaining faith rather than empty religion.

CHAPTER 7

Get Your Self-Image Right

Before my business fell apart, when my life was still operating at warp speed, I rarely stopped to think about who I was. If you had me asked me, my response would simply have been that Bill Dallas was a self-made man on the way to the top—aggressive, intelligent, and self-confident.

I was all about achievement. Mine was self-image by default, based completely on performance. I was the superstar of real estate development in the Bay Area; the fast-talking, smooth overachiever who knew no boundaries.

I was such an effective salesman that I bought my own pitch and was dedicated to ensuring that everyone else did too. But once I moved into San Quentin, I knew I had met my match. That place was packed with con artists—people whose self-images were so totally out of line with reality that they had even fooled themselves. Or, more accurately, they had *primarily* fooled themselves.

Of all the survival skills among inmates, the ability to sniff out other con artists was most common. It was probably an example of the "it takes one to know one" principle. Inmates could quickly sense a fake and see through a facade, even though they were stunningly incapable of seeing the same flaws and deceptions in themselves. I quickly learned that I would never be able to pull one over on the other inmates. They could see my act coming from a mile away.

More than most inmates, I was particularly ill-prepared to handle the San Quentin challenge. My exaggerated bravado disappeared once I was dumped inside the walls. The bad-boy party animal of the Bay Area was reduced to a wimpy, whining shadow. I was a man in crisis. My adopted self-view, vacuous as it was, no longer held up under scrutiny. And there was nothing of substance moving to the forefront to replace it.

Up to that point, I had never taken the time to look at myself in the mirror and ask tough, deep questions. But in the space of just a few months, I had gone not just from riches to rags but also from glamour man to sad sack.

- Outside the walls I had been a model for a major retail chain. Inside the walls inmates called me Clark Kent. I no longer had my contact lenses, and the prison infirmary was not equipped to replace them. I wound up with very unattractive black-rimmed glasses. The lenses were quite thick—the kind sometimes referred to as "Coke bottle lenses." (By the way, I recently learned that because optometrists can now make lenses for even the strongest prescriptions out of lighter and thinner material, eyewear like I was given is now marketed on the Internet as a novelty item, described as "black, round nerd glasses.")

- Outside the walls I lived in a beautiful, luxurious penthouse with the latest and greatest toys a man could buy. Inside the walls I shared less square footage than was available in my old bathroom. The most advanced technology in my cell was a flush toilet and running water.

- Outside the walls I always carried hundreds of dollars in my pockets. Inside the walls I was not allowed to have a single penny. Literally.

- Outside the walls my clothing was the best: expensive, stylish, impeccably tailored, and color coordinated. Inside the walls my garments were retreads from paroled inmates, patched up by the inmate tailors on the premises, and always color coordinated: blue on blue.

- Outside the walls I was the friend of every politician. Inside the walls I was a human disease that public officials could not be sufficiently inoculated against.

- Outside the walls my nights and weekends were filled with partying and sex. Inside the walls I was as dry and celibate as a monk.

- Outside the walls I was a picture of physical fitness. Inside the walls I gained thirty pounds, thanks to a consistent diet of starches and more starches, as well as an absence of any physical activity besides crying and chasing after COs to beg them to help me get out.

- Outside the walls my cars were Porsches, Jaguars, and
  BMWs. Inside the walls I hoofed it in my leather boots
  or rode in reinforced armored buses for trips to court.

Talk about a blow to my self-image! Everything that had made
me the man about town was taken away. What was I left with?
Nothing.

Once I began processing this reversal of fortune, I realized
that my story—the path of injustice and hardship that had
seemed so unique and outrageous to me—was really quite similar to the tales of the other five thousand guys sharing the San
Quentin experience with me. Sure, their crimes and backgrounds
were a bit different, but the end result for all of us was the same.

We were all serving time because we lacked character and
integrity. We had all glossed over that deficiency by adopting
a fantasy self-image. Basing our significance entirely on exter-
nals, we valued a person's life based on what he had achieved
and how the world responded to those accomplishments.

We could not have been more self-deceived.

During mealtimes and in the yard, I'd pick up bits of conversation that eventually began to penetrate through my self-
centered mental barrier. There was one phrase that really stuck
with me: "Short-timers are just Lifers on the installment plan."

As I began to pay attention to the people around me, I saw
that many of the inmates who were in for brief sentences came
back—again and again and again. Most of them would eventually wind up doing as much time as the Lifers, but with occa-
sional stretches outside the walls. They were on the installment

plan: a year on the inside, then a month out, followed by a couple of years in, then several months out, leading to a few more years in, and so forth.

I couldn't help but notice the vast difference between the Lifers and the short-timers. They generally had little to do with each other, albeit for different reasons. Short-timers generally stayed clear of the Lifers because they knew they weren't going to get any sympathy from them. Lifers refused to waste their time on foolishness. Even though they were in prison, they had learned to value every minute of every day. They had little desire to spend it playing the games of the short-timers.

Eventually I put two and two together and figured out that most short-timers had a short-term view of life, clinging desperately to a false self-image, denying that they were at fault for the crimes for which they were convicted, and waiting for the opportunity to get back to their game playing on the streets. They refused to see their character as it was, and thereby condemned themselves to committing criminal offenses over and over.

Most Lifers, on the other hand, had a long-term view of life. After a period of intensely denying their role in their circumstances and citing the injustice of their situation, most Lifers had finally taken a good, long look at themselves. After accepting responsibility for who they were and what they had done, they decided to transcend their character weaknesses. They understood that life is a gift, and they cherished every minute of it.

Kevin Hagan was a likable, articulate, dignified Lifer who

had been in the system for more than a decade. He seemed to have developed an aura of serenity and strength that enabled him to transcend the humiliating drudgery of prison life.

Although Kevin was the first to admit that he had made some serious mistakes in his life, somehow he had learned to control the thoughts and actions that got him into prison. After fighting the system for years, he realized that until he altered who he thought he was, he was powerless to change himself and how he reacted to others. This was a crucial turning point for Kevin, as it proves to be for all of us. He finally gave up control over that part of life and allowed God to initiate the transformation of his mind and heart. Over time, as God shaved off Kevin's rough edges, he abandoned his menacing, angry black man routine and adopted God's view of who Kevin Hagan really was: a man loved and gifted by God, capable of maturity, and able to exercise the self-discipline necessary to positively influence the world. The difference, he pointed out, came when he finally realized that he, along with everyone else, has innate value. He no longer felt the need to prove his value to anyone, and he no longer waited for or even expected others to earn his acceptance by proving their lives had value.

As I observed Kevin and other Lifers, I began to rethink my understanding of the audience *I* was playing to in life. For so many years, my energy had gone toward capturing the applause and appreciation of the people I wanted to impress. It had never occurred to me that the only audience that mattered was the one who created me, guided me, loved me, and held my ultimate destiny in His hand.

As a new Christian, I believed that God had made the world and that He had made me too. But the idea that my value came solely from my relationship with God—the fact that He chose to give me life, that He made me in His own image, that He loved me unconditionally, and that my life had a vital purpose within the advancement of His Kingdom—was beyond my comprehension. Each of those elements was a mind-blowing reality. Putting it all together took some time and effort, but it served as one more stepping-stone toward preparing me to be healthy.

Once I understood that I was a new creation because of my relationship with Jesus, I realized that if I truly belonged to Him, He would remake me from the inside out. My life would be new. And that meant that my self-image would be 180 degrees from where it had been before.

The idea of reconstructing my identity based on imitating and adopting the character qualities of Christ was really a life-saver for me. On my first day of prison, the system had begun the process of breaking me down, starting with my identity. I gave up my name and became a number instead. Like most inmates, I fought that process. After all, who wants to become a blank slate for the state to reprogram? But that was probably why so many short-timers returned to prison: they never abandoned their malignant self-image of the skilled, misunderstood victim of injustice at the hands of an insensitive, dehumanizing system.

But the pattern I saw among the Lifers was quite different. After their initial resistance to this process, many of them accepted the need for an image remake and moved toward a sense of self-worth that was no longer based on input from the world.

I could see that my inflated self-image and what passed for self-respect during my wild years were merely attempts to prove to myself that I mattered. If I had truly respected myself, I would not have compromised my morals to win contracts or distributed money to public officials in unethical ways. What a relief to know that the charade was over! God knew me and accepted me. I could stop pretending. I could be myself and be okay with it.

III

I don't know what your most pressing life issues are, but you might find that the approaches that helped me will also assist you in evaluating and refining your self-image.

Acknowledge the misconceptions in your self-image. My former self-image was based on factors—appearance, skills, relationships, and lifestyle—that had nothing to do with the real me. Before I could correct my view of myself I had to see my existing self-image for what it was: a lie.

Accept the fact that your value comes from God. If it is true that everything in the universe comes from and belongs to Him, then everything's ultimate worth is determined by Him too. Compliments from other people are great, but we cannot live our lives waiting for people to accept or endorse us. People are too fickle. Only God knows what we are really like, and He loves us anyway. And only He knows our true potential and does what it takes to help us reach it. I believe that is why I was in San Quentin: He was intent upon guiding me to my best self. Romans 2:29 (NLT) says, "A person with a changed heart seeks praise from God, not from people." I've had the praise of people. It vanished when the hard times arrived. But the love of God remained, whether I was cognizant of it or not.

Respect yourself, based on the value God has given you. This is harder than it sounds. Stop and listen to the way people talk to each other, bantering and bashing one another—the kind of disrespectful trash talk that has become so common in professional sports—and I think you'll agree that many of us have more self-loathing than self-love.

Some have said that we don't love ourselves because we did not receive love when we were growing up. Admittedly, a high percentage of inmates had upbringings littered with broken promises, abandonment, and parental ambivalence. Perhaps our efforts to prove that we were special and significant were just our way of compensating for the love and support we didn't get when we were younger. I'm not a psychologist— although the yard was filled with them—but I know that people often try to overcome shame or inadequacies by sheer force of will, resulting in an errant self-view. That certainly happened to me.

I had to learn to stop playing the old tapes and create new ones in my mind. In my past, I allowed that junk to play in my head all the time, and then I hung around with people who reinforced those lies. But now, the Word of God has created all new tapes that were confirmed to me by the godly people I was associating with in San Quentin.

Focus on improving your character. Putting God in the driver's seat means that we don't have to work hard to impress Him. It's a good thing, too, because none of us can impress Him. Instead, we ought to focus on improving our character—becoming more godly, not just better performers. That distinction is a tough one; it's not always easy simply to revel in our God-given value while at the same time satisfy the command from Jesus to bear fruit for His Kingdom. Sometimes the line between the two is a bit finer than we can discern, and we'll lean too heavily in one direction or the other. But the real challenge is working on the inner person. If we can get it right on the inside, we won't have to worry about what happens on the outside.

Surround yourself with people whose patterns and temperaments will help you to become a person of character. The apostle Paul's warning that "bad company corrupts good character" has probably been proven true every day since he conveyed that thought two thousand years ago (1 Corinthians 15:33). My story confirms it too. Before I went to prison, my party mates drew me into drugs, alcohol, sex, and other things that were not good for me. In prison, my time with the Lifers directed my focus to character issues and provided me with role models to learn from. I'm not perfect, but I'm much better off thanks to the good choices and solid values of these kinds of people.

If you want to get your image right, remember that once you accept Christ, you have the opportunity to shed the old ways, embrace new ones, and allow Christ to take over. As some of my inmate buddies used to say, "That's an offer you can't refuse."

Through the grace of God, I have made some progress in turning the hole in my heart into a whole heart. As much as I desire to be used by God to help transform the world, my own mind and heart must be transformed first. After all, you cannot give away what you don't possess.

TRANSFORMING PRINCIPLE
A positive self-image produces a positive life.

CHAPTER 8

Get Rid of Self-Absorption

Prison holds the world's most concentrated collection of self-absorbed people. The more time I spent listening to the conversations inside the walls, the more I realized that the only subject that generated constant attention was the speaker himself.

For the first year of my sentence, whenever I talked with other inmates, my only goal was to make sure they understood how much pain I was in. I wanted them to know just how horrible my story was. At first, some of them listened to me, but then they started to brush me off. After a while, people started to get so annoyed with me that as soon as they saw me coming toward them, they immediately turned and walked away.

I was so self-absorbed that I was alienating people, which eventually created a self-fulfilling prophecy: I believed that no one cared about me, and since I seemed to suck the life out of anyone I came in contact with, that belief was quite true.

Forget about anyone else's needs. Everything was about me: *Woe is me. What can you do for me? Poor me. What about me?*

Of course, if I had put two minutes of thought into this, I would have realized the logic in that. After all, crime is the result of someone elevating his own needs above those of the people he victimizes. Behavior always follows beliefs. Criminals generally believe that what they did was right and necessary, even if the justice system penalizes their behavior. Inmates seemed to be generally incapable of seeing the error of their ways because their frames of reference were always personal.

For instance, someone who commits armed robbery is essentially saying, "I deserve the money you earned, even if I have to traumatize you to get it." Premeditated murder is often motivated by the killer believing that the victim unjustifiably prevented the killer from fulfilling his needs or desires, which in his mind are more significant than the victim's loss of life. Arson is often undertaken out of revenge or a desire to destroy evidence—both of which send the message that the arsonist's objectives trump the value of the victims' possessions, lifestyle, time, and even their lives.

When I finished college and started working for a living in the dog-eat-dog world of business, my natural response was to pour myself into the fray and get everything I could. If everyone else was just doing whatever it took to get what they wanted, I would do the same.

But better.

And bigger.

And, of course, faster.

When I was building my real estate empire, I acted as if the world revolved around me and my dreams. My willingness to exploit people financially was my subconscious way of saying that my fame, comfort, and security mattered more than anyone else's rights or resources. My sexual exploitation of women, with lust and selfishness replacing love and commitment, was my way of taking care of my needs at the expense of whoever was the most useful resource at the moment.

In my mind, the end always justified the means. Unwittingly, I was probably the king of the Darwinists: my business philosophy was that only the strongest player survives. I played to win; there was no viable alternative. In that world, breaking the rules wasn't really wrong as long as I got away with it. Taking such risks merely demonstrated greater creativity and courage than the next guy possessed.

I was the poster child for self-absorption. My real estate deals put people's investments—sometimes representing their entire life savings—in jeopardy. My illegal fund-raising practices put public officials' careers at risk. My abuse of the public-hearing process trampled the rights and best interests of taxpayers. Not even bothering to check on the legality of my financial practices undermined the welfare of my business partner and employees.

Why did I do all of this (and more)? Because the only thing I cared about was myself: getting what I wanted, simply because I wanted it.

This Attila the Hun strategy may not be unusual in

business, but it is unbearably embarrassing for me today as a follower of Christ. Almost everything I did emerged from inappropriate motivations. But my business indiscretions were simply a reflection of a heart soiled by selfishness. My entire life reflected self-absorption, ranging from the crime of which I was convicted to mundane daily habits. My brother used to say that I had never seen a mirror that I could walk by without stopping to examine myself. There's nothing inherently wrong with looking at your reflection in a mirror—that is, after all, what they're made for—but when every moment is consumed with thoughts of yourself, you know you have a problem with self-absorption. When every choice you make hinges on how it will benefit you, it's time to give your values and perspectives a serious overhaul.

From my perspective, even the new and confusing world of San Quentin revolved around me. It took some harsh confrontations and a lot of self-reflection (yes, more think- ing about me) before such all-encompassing self-absorption became obvious and troublesome to me. When I had trans- ferred from Susanville to San Quentin, I was given a box to use for my few possessions—a few letters, my toothbrush, my glasses, etc. Although the CO was in a hurry, I was extremely concerned about my things, especially my glasses. I was afraid they might get scratched or broken, and I said as much. The guard, clearly fed up with my self-absorbed whining at this point, turned to me and said, "If you don't be quiet, you won't have to worry about those glasses anymore." And then he threatened to put them someplace that would be very uncomfortable for me. I knew better than to say anything more at that point.

A while later, as I talked with a Lifer named Michael Jordan (no, not *that* Michael Jordan), I realized that conversations with him were different from those with other inmates. For one thing, Michael always focused completely on me. That was highly unusual in prison. Usually when I talked with another inmate, especially a short-timer, I felt as if I was fighting a battle to see which one of us could grab the other's attention first in order to fill that person's ears with tales of our own personal saga and feelings.

But like most Lifers, Michael was different; he didn't play the game. In his relaxed, carefree way, he would grin and pose questions about my favorite topic: me. That was such a unique experience that it made a lasting impression and motivated me to figure out what his problem was.

His "problem," it turned out, was that Michael was no longer self-absorbed. He had surrendered his anger and selfishness several years earlier when the prison system broke him and he began a real relationship with Christ. He took seriously Paul's exhortation that we must die to self (1 Corinthians 15:31), and as a result, Michael lived for God and God's people. In the midst of the land of the self-absorbed, such selflessness was jarring.

When Michael listened to me, it had a healing effect. He was what is known as an active listener: he would hear my words, then feed them back to me both to clarify my thoughts and to push me to think more deeply or perhaps differently.

He was always engaged with my train of thought, which was affirming.

Many of my Lifer friends were like this. They had picked up some keen insights on getting over themselves. For some, the motivation was fatigue—that is, they simply got tired of listening to themselves protest the same things over and over, especially since their whining wasn't resolving their situations. At some point it also dawned on them that their fundamental way of thinking about life was what got them thrown in prison in the first place—and it was not likely to be the same thinking that would help them get out.

They also helped me see that if I wanted to escape the bondage of self-absorption, I would need to obtain and follow advice from inmates who had been around the block and earned respect. That was a big step for me. Leaning on someone else would imply that I was no longer completely self-reliant and that others might be more mature than me.

But overcoming my battle with selfishness wasn't only about replacing monologue with dialogue or taking cues from veteran inmates. That was just one part of the remedy for my disease. It was at that juncture that my faith arose as a critical factor in my transformation. Having accepted Christ as my Savior but not fully as my Lord, I had a lot of ground to cover. In my brief Christian journey, I had been taught the importance of attending church, praying, and reading and memorizing the Bible. But I had a minimal understanding of just how deeply Christ could—and should—affect my life.

If I wanted to transition from H64741, convicted felon and

sobbing loser, to Bill Dallas, maturing man of God and reborn citizen, my life's focus needed to be on God. I needed to lead a balanced life, but balance was not attainable if the chief recipient of my energy was me.

Once again, one of the Lifers embodied this principle in action. One day when Lifer Binh Vong was leaving his job at the prison industry complex, he heard a loud sound like something hitting the ground hard. He turned around and saw a CO on the ground. For some reason, this officer had been up in one of the trees in the yard and the branch he was on broke. He fell, and the branch hit him on the back.

When Binh first saw him, the officer was on the ground, moaning, obviously in pain. Other inmates who were nearby saw what happened and just watched and laughed, but Binh was focused on the CO. Without thinking, he ran over toward the guard, yelling for help as he ran. He bent down over the fallen officer, and in a matter of seconds, other officers began to respond, even the special security unit that is the prison equivalent of a SWAT team. It wasn't unusual to see the Goon Squad—as they were known among inmates—dressed in full riot gear, ready for dramatic, violent action. Their job was to break up gangs and drug rings, and to eliminate any other type of illegal activity taking place within the walls. They were not known for their gentleness or sensitivity.

The officers' first instinct was to assume that Binh was trying to stab or beat up the CO. They surrounded him, weapons raised. Binh knew that fighting back would be futile, so he just covered his face with his hands and prepared to be beaten.

Suddenly the hurt officer yelled out, "Don't touch him! He was the one who helped me!" Binh couldn't believe his ears. No blows had been struck yet. He was still curled up in a protective position when they pulled him to his feet, guns still trained on him. The injured CO repeated the instruction that Binh not be harmed, reaffirming that he had helped him. Notes were made about the incident, and the officers brought Binh back to his cell unharmed.

Some time later prison officials investigated the incident, and the lieutenant in charge told Binh he was very lucky that he wasn't killed. In fact, the investigation revealed that the officer on duty in the gun tower overlooking the yard that day had fallen asleep! If he had been awake and doing his job, there's a good chance that Binh would have been shot that day.

But the best part of his story was yet to come.

Binh had had more than his fair share of encounters with the parole board. Like most Lifers, Binh had been up for parole numerous times—eleven times, to be exact—and had been denied each time. By the time of this incident, he had already served more than twenty years. It seems that his rejections were political in nature, but he never really knew the reasons behind the decisions. Parole was never a sure thing, but being denied was enough to cause major heartbreak. I could not imagine what it would have been like for Binh to anticipate his release eleven times, only to have the dream destroyed each time. Maintaining hope for the future became more difficult with each subsequent denial. Yet it hadn't stopped him from stepping in to help the CO.

He finally was given a parole date. That date is typically awarded by the board three to six months in advance of the release day because the approval has to work its way through the state government bureaucracy, eventually being approved by the governor. In this case, Binh received his date, only to have it withdrawn a few months later by the governor. Crestfallen, Binh appealed the reversal.

The appeal was held in Sacramento, the state's capital, and Binh's attorneys were there to make his case. But the words that spoke the loudest were those of the CO Binh had aided after the tree accident. Of his own volition, that officer showed up at the appeal hearing and spoke on Binh's behalf. He ended his emotional narrative by saying, "Binh Vong saved my life." The story touched everybody in that room.

Three days later he was released from prison.

The angry young Binh who had entered prison years ago would not have given a second thought to an officer who fell out of a tree. But his extended time behind the walls had given him the opportunity to slow down, find himself, and reconsider his life philosophy. In the course of those reflections he changed his views of people—and himself. Binh explains it best: "Finally, I saw that people have value, whether they're wearing blue [inmates] or green [officers]."

Binh's courageous and compassionate act toward the CO was exactly the kind of selfless behavior that I had to learn while in San Quentin. Men like Binh, serving life sentences for their past mistakes, became my teachers. It is that kind of selfless behavior that Jesus encouraged His followers to exhibit when He said, "Whoever finds his life will lose it, and whoever loses his life for my sake will find it" (Matthew 10:39).

III

Somewhere along the way, many of us have accepted pop culture's mandates to "take care of number one" and to "look out for yourself because nobody else will." It's easy to buy into these concepts without thoughtful examination.

Don't misunderstand: I'm not advocating self-loathing as the solution. Some degree of self-love is not only natural but necessary. But some people—like me and my fellow inmates—go way overboard. We fail to realize that if the only thing you truly love and care about is yourself, you can never attain the fulfillment that self-absorption seeks to satisfy.

In an effort to keep my own level of self-absorption in check, I developed a little inventory of questions. You might find them helpful too. These six questions are rather ordinary, but the answers can produce a powerful restorative effect in your life.

QUESTION 1: Who is the primary focus of the conversations in which I participate?

QUESTION 2: How well do I know the people with whom I spend the most time?

QUESTION 3: In my daily agenda, whose needs am I focused on satisfying?

QUESTION 4: What is the focus of my life vision?

QUESTION 5: How much time do I devote to praying for the needs of others each day?

QUESTION 6: How often do people seek me out for advice or counsel?

Regularly addressing these simple questions keeps me from falling back into the it's-all-about-me pattern.

Jesus regularly implored people to keep their eyes off themselves and on God and others. He also said that the most important pair of commandments were to love God with all our hearts, minds, strength, and soul, and to love others as much as we love ourselves (Mark 12:29-31). Naturally, if our hearts are invested in God and other people, there won't be much time or energy left over to obsess about ourselves.

Paul promoted the same idea from a different angle. He warned the Philippians not to be selfish, show off, or think they were better or more important than others. He told them to take an interest in other people and have the same focus as Jesus, which was on God the Father and fellow human beings. A related theme that runs throughout the New Testament is that of serving people. Doing so shifts the center of our attention from our own desires to the needs of other people. That mentality certainly drove Binh to the side of the fallen CO, and it motivated many of the Lifers I knew to befriend and encourage me in my journey to wholeness.

How ironic that the Lifers were doing time because they

had broken society's laws but were now the best examples I had encountered of men living in strict accordance with God's laws. They truly captured the essence of Christ's command that we love other people as much as we love ourselves.

Our time on earth is not about extracting maximum self-satisfaction. We were purchased at a price for the benefit and purposes of a loving God who is calling us to love and serve a needy human race. Keep your eyes focused on God and others, and your life will have meaning beyond anything the world has to offer.

TRANSFORMING PRINCIPLE

True fulfillment will never result from a life of self-absorption.

CHAPTER 9

Shape Your Attitude

Inside the walls of San Quentin, there was nothing I craved
more than freedom. I had taken it for granted for three
decades. Now I needed it like a junkie needs his drug fix.
When I arrived at the prison, I began counting down the
number of days until I would be eligible for parole. The days
dragged on interminably, agonizing minute after agonizing
minute. Freedom seemed to be an eternity away.

But what I did not yet realize was that freedom is not a
physical space I could occupy or even the ability to dictate my
own schedule. True freedom is all about attitude.

Many things contributed to my attitude about my
imprisonment. Improper expectations were one element,
and I harbored more than my fair share. I had expected
everyone to rally to my defense at the injustice of my being
thrown into San Quentin. I had a whole litany of complaints:
The cells were too small, the beds were uncomfortable, and
we were not allowed to have pillows. The toilet was just

inches—inches!—from my head. The food was barely fit for human consumption. The clothing didn't fit properly. The guards made too much noise during their rounds at night. I couldn't go when and where I wanted. Showering was a nightmare. Who thought up this torture?

It hadn't penetrated my brain that this was *prison*. My expectations were out of line, so naturally my attitude was awful. My expectations might have been reasonable for a free person—although even that is somewhat questionable—but they were certainly unreasonable for a convicted felon.

Month after month of narrowly focusing on my own situation had kept me in a prison inside the prison—the confines of my own mind. As long as I maintained that attitude, I was doomed to a life sentence.

In San Quentin, attitude was palpable. Some inmates used their attitude as one more defense against a hostile environment. It was such a big deal that San Quentin even had three special places designed to "adjust" people's attitudes—the Administrative Segregation Unit (known as AdSeg, where the repentant are prepared to return to the mainline), the Adjustment Center (for those whose truly hard-core attitudes need to be broken), and the Segregated Housing Unit (most commonly referred to as the Hole, for the most severe offenses).

A major part of the prison experience was dedicated to adjusting an inmate's head. Sometimes the process was wonderfully effective. Most of the Lifers I came to know and respect—and to rely upon for my own attitude adjustment—

had transitioned from hostile to hospitable during their stay in San Quentin.

The Lifers who coached me through my sentence lacked physical freedom but had achieved personal freedom in their minds, hearts, and spirits. The fact that they were behind bars was irrelevant. They were free no matter what the warden or the State of California proclaimed. Their freedom just happened to exist on the wrong side of the walls.

During my frenetic days in real estate—when I thought I was free—I had never encountered anyone quite like these Lifers. They had an inner peace unlike anything I had ever seen— or recognized, at least. That peace came from their decision to accept life for what it was. Just as Paul instructed the Colossians to transcend the mundane issues of daily life by setting their minds on eternal matters (Colossians 3:1-3), these Lifers had figured out that they could be free if they didn't focus on the things that sought to limit or destroy them. It was all a matter of choices and attitude.

Once my turnaround began, the Lifers were instrumental in facilitating and cementing my attitude shift. After being in San Quentin for about six months, something really seemed to click for me. I realized that I was no longer Bill Dallas, San Quentin prisoner. I was Bill Dallas, friend of the Lifers. Doing time suddenly became so much easier. I was an inmate, and I was proud to be part of this community of men who had become my friends and my family.

This was a monumental shift for me. Suddenly I started seeing everything differently: myself, others, and even my situation.

Kevin Hagan was one of those life-giving felons. Kevin's mantra was this: "You can lock my body up, but you can't lock up my mind, you can't lock up my heart, and you can't lock up my spirit."

Kevin was constantly checking on me, asking me how I was doing and if there was anything I needed. He always seemed to have a smile on his face, and I loved to be around him because his spirit was so positive. He was just happy to be alive.

This was a new perspective for me. Here we were in San Quentin, a maximum-security prison. Everything around us seemed negative to me. I felt as if the world owned me and I was helpless to do anything about it. But although Kevin had every reason to be miserable, he refused to let his situation dictate his character or how he felt about life. He believed that it was his responsibility to help the next guy, and I'm so thankful for that since I happened to be that next guy.

We all could have given up. But Kevin—and, eventually, I—realized that the way we dealt with San Quentin was up to us. In fact, the way we dealt with life was up to us.

Like Kevin, the Lifers were constantly teaching me about attitude—not by lecturing me, but by modeling transformational attitudes themselves.

Sam Green* had been both a feared and a fearless man when he entered San Quentin. His attitude fueled the fierce anger that caused him to be moved from prison to prison.

---

* Sam's name has been changed to protect his privacy.

Those who knew him when he first arrived quickly learned to watch themselves when he was around. No one dared say anything against him—or even to him. If they did, he would stab them, no questions asked.

But after years of anger and hostility, Sam was transformed into one of the most dynamic, authentic Christians I had ever met. His foundation in Christ was so strong it seemed that nothing could shake him. Like many others, Sam had finally reached a place where he realized that his anger and hate would only destroy him. He realized that the Christ who died for him was also the Christ who loved him, and he surrendered his life totally to God.

It was hard for me to imagine that Sam had ever been someone to be feared. I had seen the way that he consoled inmates when they were discouraged or down, and he was known for his hugs. Sam had already served twenty years when I met him, and he had been rejected for parole fifteen times. There was no guarantee that he would ever get out. But he was always focused on the positive, believing that God must have more work for him to do for his fellow inmates in San Quentin.

Just like Sam, Michael Jordan had entered prison as an angry, hostile man but eventually became someone who would give you the shirt off his back without hesitation. I cannot count how many days big Michael—who was well over six feet tall and a good 250 pounds, much of which was muscle—sat down and talked with me, lifting my spirits and giving me positive affirmation and hope. Even when my only response was whining, he never stopped smiling and gently leading me to a new vantage point. He and others like him helped save my life.

The more time I spent with the Lifers, the more I realized the importance of befriending positive people. While I was in San Quentin, I was constantly being moved around for various reasons—or sometimes for what seemed no reason at all. I stayed in many different cells, in four different cell blocks. And in some of those cells I had several cellies come and go. One of them, Terry, was memorable only because he was such a downer. The only thing he could talk about was how lousy his life was, how it was everyone else's fault, how the system was bringing him down, and how someday he'd get back at "the Man."

When Terry and I shared a cell, I wasn't exactly Mr. Sunshine, either. But Terry was like audio poison: I could only listen for a few minutes before I had to tune him out. I always wondered how he was able to maintain such dense pessimism and futility, and then I realized that the entire group of short-timers he hung around with also saw only the negative side of life. They spurred each other on to greater and greater depths of despair and discouragement. Terry was the most negative person I had ever met—even worse than I had been. If you had asked the inmates who was the most pathetic person in the yard, the answer would have been Terry. A few months earlier, I would have been a close second. Thankfully, I had experienced an attitude shift, though living with him gave me a snapshot of the direction my life could have gone if I had not experienced such a turnaround.

Terry used crutches to help him walk, though I was pretty sure he didn't really need them. I often saw him walk around the cell or in the shower, but as soon as he was out in the general population, he would use them. Those physical crutches were symbolic of the attitude of defeatism that Terry leaned on in his life. He didn't really need it to survive, but he had become so accustomed to it, he really didn't know how to function any other way.

Because I was getting better, I could see that Terry was the epitome of what negativity could become in a person's life. I felt sorry for Terry because I realized that he couldn't see past his own problems.

It was actually Vy's story that played a key role in opening my eyes to the importance of focusing on the positive. When Vy Le was first thrown in prison, he was beyond rage over his circumstances. He was an unruly inmate and was transferred from prison to prison. His inner strength, fueled by his rage, pushed him to never back down. He verbally abused the guards, fought with other inmates, and generally caused trouble wherever he was. It got so bad that they eventually threw him in the Hole for eighteen months. Eighteen months!

The Hole was no picnic. Locked in an isolated area of the prison, Vy was allowed no privileges at all: no family visits, jobs, inmate interaction, library books, or the like. His time outside the cell was extremely limited; even his meals were pushed under his cell door. Sometimes he wasn't allowed out at all for a week or more.

When the guards woke Vy up each morning, he had to

roll up his mattress and put it outside the cell door. That left him alone in a small cell with a metal bed frame, a toilet, and a sink. The only clothing he was given was boxer shorts, a T-shirt, and socks. On shower days he was cuffed, and the guards shuffled him down the corridor to a special cell that was set up for showers. He was then locked in that cell and his cuffs were removed. He was allowed a brief shower before he was recuffed and shuffled back to his cell.

The Hole had one purpose: attitude adjustment. It had a surprisingly efficient record of breaking down even the toughest of the tough guys.

And Vy spent a year and a half in that place. My blood runs cold just thinking about it. Fortunately, it did the trick with him. Miraculously, God penetrated the security of the place and the hardness of Vy's heart and began a long process of changing his attitude. God was slowly healing Vy of all the pain and poison that controlled his mind and heart. It was the beginning of a process that would take years, but one that would produce the most authentic follower of Christ I have ever known.

Vy eventually got rid of his anger, replacing it with a positive outlook. And most importantly, Vy emerged from the Hole a different person because he had reflected on his life and embraced the trials he had encountered. Central to that reformation was Vy's realization that as long as those hardships embittered him, they controlled him. Recalling the wonderful years of his early childhood, he concluded that he was made for something better than hatred and hostility.

When Vy walked out of the Hole and returned to the block, you could not help but notice the difference. For one thing, he had regained his bright, toothy smile. And beyond that, he was a man who was transferring his internal strength into an attitude of deep inner peace. He acknowledged that he had messed up big-time and that he could rebuild his life if he accepted responsibility for his past and his future. And he did. He became a model inmate, one of the most popular men in San Quentin, and he invested time in a relationship with God that continued to produce an attitude of joy and peace.

Through Vy, I realized that I had this same opportunity. Once it became clear that it was up to me to see the glass either as half-empty or half-full, I realized I had two choices: I could continue to plead my case as a victim of life to anyone who would listen to my sad saga, or I could see my life as a beautiful and adventurous gift from God and live it to the fullest. It was up to me whether I spent my time trying to convince people of the injustice of my situation or becoming the solution to my dilemma. I could decide to give up in weakness or to fight back with God's strength.

III

What's the big deal about attitude? Almost everyone in maximum-security facilities lands there because of serious attitude problems. Some inmates are there because they committed crimes out of disrespect and arrogance. Some were motivated by hatred or anger. Others were either intolerant or selfish. In each case, however, their attitudes affected their judgment, which led to inappropriate behavior and imprisonment.

Let's face it; life is hard. To succeed you have to think, you cannot just react. My shallow Christianity failed me early on because it was too superficial; mine was a lazy, inch-deep faith. I saw no parallels between what Jesus taught about character and my own situation. Though I had memorized numerous passages of Scripture, I had not grasped their true significance because I hadn't learned to wring the full meaning out of them.

From watching the Lifers master their attitudinal challenges, I knew that appropriate choices can be made, even after a prolonged span of bad attitudinal choices. Even my own brief journey proved that anyone can make the transition from the dark side to a more upbeat perspective. Consider the following keys that were instrumental in my own turnaround.

Focus on character rather than on circumstances. During my real estate years, my attitude had been based on a combination of unrealistic expectations and a narrow interpretation of my life's circumstances. My attitude was easy to read but hard to predict because it was completely based on my immediate situation. I was up one moment, down the next. When things were going well—which meant I was satisfying my financial and leisure goals—my attitude was upbeat and positive. When things took a turn for the worse—meaning my business was suffering or my party life was stalled—my attitude went south. When my business crashed and my life went down the tubes, my attitude went down with it. Because

I didn't have a strong character to lean on, I was wholly reliant on the superficial—my attitudes were based on vague perceptions and gut reactions to circumstances.

When I accepted Christ in the middle of the storm, the roots of my faith were shallow. The television preacher had said something that became a kind of mantra for me: "God and I will be okay." Cheesy as it sounds now, in my foggy state of mind, it passed for profound wisdom. Based on the assumption that God would smooth out the details and I'd be on my way back to the top in no time, my attitude became more optimistic.

But once I was taken away in handcuffs, the superficiality and denial that had sustained me through the courtroom embarrassments evaporated. Instantly, everything in life appeared dark and gloomy. I could not imagine anything good ever happening to me again. Fueled by an attitude of depression and despair, I believed that the world was out to get me. God was no longer a perfect, loving deity; if He was, why would He shatter me like this?

It took me a long time to understand that the power to transcend my conditions had always been available to me through Christ. I had to abandon my morose attitude before He would partner with me to get me to a better place.

Choose a positive outlook. Attitude is not a product of circumstances; it is always a choice that we make. It is not handed down without any possibility of change; it is something we determine for ourselves. As author and speaker Chip Ingram explains, you can't always change your circumstances, but you can change your perspective. In fact, he uses this formula: circumstances plus perspective equals experience. Your perspective creates your experience.

The Lifers had intuitively grasped the substance of this formula. The short-timers, on the other hand, had mastered the downer attitude. Their arguments were always the same: Nothing is fair. Everyone is out to get me. God shortchanged me. I really believe that inmates with this kind of attitude are destined to return to prison because their attitude virtually demands it.

In the same way, a lot of people who will never serve time in prison are locked up in personal prisons inside their own heads. Their stubborn refusal to break free of negative thinking resigns them to a life of morose complaining and agonizing. It doesn't take Sherlock Holmes to find people who are drowning in self-pity and won't even try to transcend their hardships. Perhaps you face some very difficult circumstances too. Remember that the choice of how you see and respond to those circumstances is completely up to you. You can choose to stand up to your trials and defeat them, or you can choose to cry foul and let those conditions defeat you. Only you can make that choice.

Replace fear with hope. One of the greatest causes of a bad attitude is fear. We all struggle with fears, and sometimes they are legitimate. But when we let fear control us, it warps our vision of everything and everybody. Some inmates I was in prison with were angry or hostile because they feared their sentence conveyed that they were losers. Others feared their weaknesses or insecurities would be revealed. A few got into trouble because they feared success. No matter what the fear is, it can corrupt your attitude overnight.

For me, fear had been ever present. Growing up, I lived in a home filled with tension and fear magnified by the general dysfunction of my family. When I did something wrong or displeasing, my father would yell at my mother, "He's the monster you created." (I didn't fully appreciate the meaning of that until years later when I discovered he was not my biological father.) It was as if my parents assumed I was going to be a failure, and they were insulating themselves from that eventuality.

During my teen years, fear was even at the root of my religious involvement. Having consistently failed my parents, I discovered that I had been failing God all along as well—and that He was a God of wrath who would not tolerate such disobedience and disappointment. It was fear of His reprisal that drove me to constant prayer and gut-wrenching anxiety about my eternal destiny.

All of this negativity and fear created a tape that played over and over in my mind, pointing out my ignorance, my inabilities, and every other shortcoming. Winding up in San Quentin simply proved the tape had been right all along. I made good on my own long-held fear.

But when I looked at the Lifers, I realized that many of them had come from equally dysfunctional backgrounds, and they had less education and more strikes against them than I had. Yet they had made an active choice to focus on hope. They saw that there were two roads to go down, and they chose the right one. I, too, needed to make a conscious effort to turn away from fear and toward hope.

Surround yourself with positive people. A lot of inmates adopt bad attitudes because they hang out with other inmates who have bad attitudes. It's very tough to break free from your environment. That's why kids whose parents are in jail often wind up in jail; it's what they know. The power of an environment filled with bad attitudes is overwhelming; it sucks you in and holds you captive.

Of course, the power of a room full of positive attitudes is equally stunning. One of the life lessons I took from San Quentin is the importance of choosing the right friends. If the attitudes of the people you spend time with are optimistic and morally righteous, the chances of you having such an attitude is tremendously improved.

In my case, getting to know and learn from the likes of Vy, Sam, Michael, Kevin, and other Lifers boosted my attitude to a place it never would have gone otherwise. They modeled proper behavior, but they also shaped my frame of mind.

Keep things in perspective. Many inmates land in prison because they cannot assess the scope of a statement or behavior. Hundreds of inmates were in prison during my tenure because they allowed minor irritations to expand into major problems, and their response was way out of proportion. Anyone who considers all experiences to be of equal magnitude and significance is asking for trouble. Not many prisoners are familiar with the expression "Don't sweat the small stuff; by the way, it's all small stuff." Even fewer would understand it.

Why waste time moaning about how lousy life is when you could just as easily acknowledge and take advantage of all the terrific aspects and opportunities it presents? The Lifers and short-timers saw life through very different lenses and, in turn, handled their sentences very differently. Clearly the Lifers had the upper hand. It was obvious in the way they carried themselves: their walk, speech, posture, behavior, and even facial expressions.

Live in the moment. If you pick up the daily newspaper and read the stories, it's easy to get down. War, political corruption, debt, inflation, murder, droughts, global warming, food shortages, poverty, drugs—the list of problems and crises is endless. But in your present reality, what do you see and touch? What is real to you, personally? Is it an intriguing challenge on the job? Maybe the beauty and pleasure brought by your children? Could it be a chance to relax in your comfortable home? Do you experience good health? Whatever your circumstances may be, you make the choice to focus on the wonderful components in your immediate presence or to build up anxieties about things you cannot control. When Jesus told His disciples to worry only about today because future troubles could not be addressed now, He was imploring His followers to live in the moment—and to enjoy it for what it was (Matthew 6:25-34).

Think about what it means to be a follower of Christ. Having a relationship with Him, knowing that your salvation has been handed to you as an undeserved gift, being given the words of God Himself to guide you through life, being surrounded by a local community of fellow Christ lovers, experiencing His presence through genuine worship—well, you get the picture. Shouldn't that alone raise your spirits?

One of the most riveting spectacles you could ever see is a group of tough-looking, albeit softhearted, Lifers speaking to an arrogant group of young hoodlums brought to the prison through programs like Scared Straight. The young gangsters enter the gates in full swagger, trying to convince a house of five thousand certified bad boys that they are too tough for words. The Lifers give their perspective on life and prison, and before the first hour expires, true fear seizes many of these young wannabes. What's most chilling of all is that the words that dissolve the confidence of these visiting gangsters are not exaggerated by the Lifers for effect; they are simply stating truths about prison life.

The Lifers do those presentations because they care about young people. Their attitudes are not like those of the short-timers, which run along the lines of "let those punks see if they'd last a day in here." The Lifers hold life in such high regard that they do whatever they can to prevent the ignorant or the arrogant bad boys of society from throwing their lives away for nothing. These Lifers demonstrate the attitude of a servant, perhaps the last thing you would expect to find among convicted killers, rapists, and arsonists.

So put a few of these different attitude derailers together—inappropriate expectations, lazy thinking, negative-minded friends, fear, distorted perspective—and before you know it, you're a train wreck waiting to happen. What's worse is that a bad attitude feeds on itself; it seduces you until you are hooked. Escaping its clutches takes an act of courage and determination.

Many of us live in prisons. Some of us are imprisoned by the ravages of bad health, others by an insufferable marriage or a wayward child, or perhaps a job that we dislike but must stick with because of the money or benefits. But in a way, even these are prisons of our own making. While we may not have any control over our circumstances, the solution to these dilemmas is really a change in attitude more than anything else. Quadriplegics cope with their condition by changing their attitudes. Marriages are saved by partners who shift their attitudes. Jobs become tolerable when we change our attitudes about them.

Jesus taught this truth when He talked about seeking peace internally, not through the events and circumstances in which we find ourselves. "Peace I leave with you; my peace I give you. I do not give to you as the world gives. Do not let your hearts be troubled and do not be afraid" (John 14:27). If we focus on our troubles, they will rule us. But if we focus on our blessings and on God, we will find inner peace.

When Jesus said the truth would set us free, He was describing not just factual accuracy or even His death and resurrection on our behalf. His message was that truth could rescue our troubled minds from unnecessary stress and anxiety. Only when we rest in the unfolding of God's grand plan can we find lasting freedom.

One day I had an enlightening conversation with one of the veteran prison guards. I asked him what would happen if an earthquake hit the area—we were in northern California, after all—and the fortress walls crumbled.

"No question about it," the lieutenant said with quiet authority. "Every short-timer in here would run for the hills like there was no tomorrow. The predators would be giving them a run for their money. Death row guys would be shufflin' out of the gates in their ankle restraints as fast as they could."

We shared a laugh at the mental image of all those men in blue denim running the fastest sprint of their lives. "And the Lifers who have made peace with themselves," he continued, "would stay right here. They wouldn't run. In fact, I'd bet that most of them would immediately search through the rubble to help the injured. They know they'll leave this place when their time is up. They'll walk out the front door with dignity."

His answer to my simple question surprised me. Over the next few days, that conversation dominated my thoughts. I reflected on the character of the Lifers I knew and concluded that the lieutenant was right.

When you get your attitude right, you can handle anything the world throws at you. Even life in prison.

TRANSFORMING PRINCIPLE
Sometimes a good attitude adjustment can save your life.

CHAPTER 10

Give Respect

The first time a fight broke out in the prison yard and inmates started dropping to the ground, I was perplexed. I heard shots, and I had no idea what was going on. But I had been in prison long enough to know that my best bet was to follow the behavior of those around me. In this case, it seemed that everyone was on the ground, lying facedown. The idea of lying on that ground and putting my face down in the dirt was repulsive to me. One of the most common habits of inmates was spitting. They were *constantly* spitting. And now I was supposed to jump into that pool of saliva? But I knew it was a matter of survival: I could endure the filth or I could get shot. Even in my befuddled state of mind, that wasn't too tough of a decision.

It didn't take long for me to figure out the protocol following a fight in the yard. As soon as a fight broke out, the guards fired a warning shot into the air. That was our signal to get prostrate on the ground as quickly as possible, facing down and not moving. That allowed the guards to see who was fighting—the combatants were so intent upon slugging each other that they didn't hear the shots and were the only ones left standing. The guards then hustled over to cuff them, remove them from the area, and place them in lockdown. In later situations, I learned that if, for some reason, people *didn't* hit the ground, shots would be fired into the entanglement of bodies until the guards were able to get matters under control.

Every society has its code of behavior. In most cultures, from tribal societies to highly developed nations, respect is the most basic response that you give to another person. The prison code is no different: when you steal someone's respect, you have seriously injured that person and can expect to pay for it in one way or another. In almost every case, fights in San Quentin were the result of seriously disrespectful behavior. Inmates defended their dignity because it was such a precious commodity in an environment where there was little else of value. For prisoners who had been stripped of everything— including our names—the only thing that remained was our self-respect and our human dignity.

Possessing nothing else, we did what we could to protect and keep that respect. It became the initial foundation for rebuilding our lives. Because human life was not always highly regarded by prisoners, respect was not automatically given—it had to be earned. It wasn't hard to do, but I realized that the effort to do so must be intentional and consistent.

Once in a great while, the prison offered us a chance to get out of our cells for a movie day. On one particular occasion, we had gathered in one of the prison's big classrooms to watch one of my favorites, *Stand and Deliver*. I had always loved that movie, and I started getting really annoyed when one of the bigger guys in the room started whispering to the inmate next to him.

I leaned over, touched his arm lightly, and *politely* asked him to stop talking to his friend.

Fatal mistake.

The guy turned to me, and the look in his eyes said in no uncertain terms, *You are going to die.*

I was scared to death, and I knew that I'd never be able to enjoy the rest of the movie. I thought maybe I should try to patch things up, but when I tried to apologize, it only made things worse. I'm not sure why he decided to let me live; maybe because he figured I wasn't worth his time. Whatever the reason, I definitely learned the importance of respecting others—even when I felt like they weren't respecting me.

Of course, there *were* some things that automatically got respect in prison. For instance, we knew better than to ask another prisoner to discuss his crime. Ever. We also avoided making any remarks about an inmate's race or heritage. We never voiced a disparaging comment about someone else's family members. We did not intrude into his space without permission, and we did not borrow his belongings. The mere existence of these unspoken rules suggested to me that God has indeed placed in our hearts the ability to respect other people. The question is whether or not we choose to acknowledge that inner compass and follow those guidelines.

I wish I could say that I understood all of this when I

arrived in San Quentin, but no etiquette manual was distributed to new residents. Though I was hardly rational when I arrived, I was alert enough to learn how to survive by watching what others did and following their example. Even though mine was not a life sentence, I had seen enough to know that my best strategy was to follow the Lifers.

I talked to Vy Le about this matter of respect, and he emphasized one of the primary lessons prison taught him. "When I came to prison, I had no respect for anyone. I was angry and believed everyone was out to get me and was just looking out for themselves. But then I came to realize that everyone is a child of God, trying to get the respect of others. I realized that in God's eyes we are all just children. I had to grow up and understand that all people have value because God loves them. If I do not show them respect, I am not giving them what God wants me to give them. It is my responsibility to show every person respect, whether I feel like it or not. This was very humbling to me."

I had similar conversations with other Lifers—some who were convicted murderers. These men told me that once they understood the concept of respect, it radically changed their thinking, and because of that, they would never kill a person again. That choice was not a reflection of their disdain for prison; it was a product of their newfound appreciation for the value of human life. These Lifers wanted their own lives to be restored because they now treasured the things they had taken for granted before: life, family, and God-given opportunities to help others. In the process of thinking about life and what matters, they had concluded that life is, in fact, a precious gift from God, and every human being deserves respect.

Before I came to prison, I didn't have a lot of respect for anyone. I saw people only for what they could give me. I assumed I was higher on the totem pole than most people, and therefore I deserved to be treated with respect—not the other way around.

Even when I came to prison, I considered myself superior to the other inmates. I was better educated and came from a better socioeconomic background. If I hadn't respected anyone outside the walls, surely I wasn't going to respect anyone inside the walls.

Ironically, the first people I ever learned to respect were the Lifers of San Quentin—the supposed worst of the worst. And in turn, I learned to respect others. And for the first time, I learned to respect myself.

The more I watched the Lifers, the more I realized the importance of this principle. Most of them seemed to assume the unofficial role of mentor to the youngsters—their name for the young short-timers—teaching them how to be men rather than punks. They knew that most of the guys who had short sentences were not seeking to become better human beings. They simply wanted to serve their time, get out of prison, and get back to their lives. The Lifers, however, understood that one of the reasons the youngsters were in jail in the first place—and one of the reasons for their high recidivism rate— was their lack of respect for others. So Lifers did what they could to train the short-timers to give due respect.

When a short-timer said or did something that was out of line, the Lifers would normally ignore it; they refused even to acknowledge the existence of the youngster. When I asked them why they didn't respond more directly, the Lifers explained that the offender was "just stupid" or "foolish" and didn't deserve the dignity of an acknowledgment or a respectful reply. They would not endanger their parole status or their reputation by fighting against a disrespectful youngster; they had too much self-respect to stoop that low. It would take an extreme offense for a Lifer to respond violently. I did see such a reaction a couple of times and quickly realized that I never wanted to be on the receiving end of that response; once they were pushed over that edge because their dignity had been violated, they felt they had nothing to lose and would fight to the death if necessary to even the score.

Interestingly, the guards also understood this principle of respect. Contrary to what I first assumed about the prison guards, I found most of them to be decent people. If we treated them with respect, they returned it. On the whole, prison officers seemed supportive of inmates being rehabilitated, and they knew that a person required respect in order to start down the path of rehabilitation.

The guards did not allow short-timers to disrespect the Lifers. They knew that Lifers set the pace and helped to maintain control and standards inside the walls. Without fanfare, the Lifers regularly informed the guards of any short-timers who were causing or seemed likely to cause problems. This was not ratting out the bad guys as much as it was an act of preserving peace among the prison population. Prison officials did their best to provide a place where inmates could be rehabilitated and then returned to society as good citizens; anyone who threatened the equilibrium could have a negative influence on the lives of others. Those youngsters were typically transferred to another prison within a day or two of having been singled out by a trusted Lifer in order to prevent significant issues from erupting. Lifers had enough respect for the system and for their own freedom that they accepted this task.

III

Every day I witness acts of disrespect, some more flagrant than others, but all significant in their own right. Have you ever considered the following things to be disrespectful?

- Smoking, swearing, or littering in public locations
- Saying rude or inappropriate things about other people, especially when they are not present to hear those remarks
- Assuming that someone is incapable of accomplishing a specific task simply because of race, ethnicity, gender, or age
- Using a cell phone in a theater during a movie or in a church during a service
- Exploiting employees by refusing to give them appropriate benefits or opportunities
- Making rude or untrue comments about public leaders, such as the president or members of Congress

- Interrupting someone while he or she is talking because you want to be sure to make your own point

The list could go on and on. We have become desensitized to such acts of disrespect, and as a result, we reap the consequences of being a nation of arrogant, self-focused people. When you lose respect for others, you diminish the value of your own dignity.

Our society seems to have lost a large share of its knowledge of etiquette. In the old days, manners were taught and reinforced by every social institution—family, schools, and church. Today, families do shockingly little to teach and enforce manners; schools believe behavioral shaping is not their responsibility; churches are just happy to have people show up. The result is that young people are not being taught the ways of showing respect to others—and, of course, knowing how to behave in order to earn respect.

No wonder our prisons are overflowing, with one out of every ninety-nine adults incarcerated—the highest proportion in the world.[4] Too few people are willing to take responsibility for teaching children the importance and the practices of giving and earning respect. The short-timers in San Quentin demonstrated flagrant disregard for the rights of others: they made noise at all hours of the day and night, they used vulgar language wherever they were, they pushed every limit related to people's dignity and self-respect. My sense, however, is that they were just the ones who were caught committing a crime; their behavior is really indicative of entire generations that have dismissed the boundaries of respect.

Consider the following keys to becoming more respectful, and in turn, earning the respect of others.

Recognize that every human life has value. As Christians, it is important to always give respect, whether we get it back or not. Because we are creatures of God, we have inherent value. To withhold respect from another person is to devalue that person's life. Even during His darkest moments—illegal trials, insulting conversations, beatings—Jesus always gave people the respect they deserved as human beings.

Learn to control your tongue. Before entering San Quentin, I was a bit of a wise guy: quick-witted, sharp-tongued, never at a loss for words. But while I was there, I learned that controlling the tongue is the first step toward giving people respect. Of course, that's a biblical principle, too; James describes the tongue as the match that can set a forest ablaze, an untamable instrument of either blessing or corruption (James 3:3-12).

The Lifers were men of few words, but their speech was usually intentional and authoritative. Many of them were in prison because of their inability to control their mouths; but after years of training, they had learned that less is more. However, they also knew that giving respect was more than simply watching their words. It all starts with a proper perception of human life, recognizing that as God's prized creation we each have dignity and deserve respect.

Listen when others speak. People who give respect listen intently and completely to what others have to say. They do not interrupt. The Lifers somehow had learned this behavior, perhaps because they realized that every word spoken has value and deserves consideration. Interrupting someone who is speaking is rude and a show of disrespect. Often we do so because we are rushed and feel we don't have time to allow someone to offer a full argument. That simply underscores the benefit of leading a simpler, less frantic life. Eliminating the time pressure seems to facilitate the patience that allows us to be fully respectful of others.

Respect is one of those areas where you can test yourself pretty easily. Take a day this week and train yourself to review each conversation after it has been completed. Evaluate how many times you interrupted the other person, for whatever reason. Could you do better? Or maybe try this: reflect on each conversation you had and count the times when you were only half listening—just enough to get by. Again, could you improve how often you fully devote your attention to the person you are speaking with?

Establish clear boundaries. When it comes to respect, we have to establish boundaries and then consistently adhere to them. If someone is generally disrespectful, it is in my own best interest to disassociate myself from that person. As a follower of Christ, I hope to have a positive influence on the lives of others, but sometimes I can best do so from a comfortable distance rather than through intimacy.

Lifers coached youngsters out of lifestyles of disrespect by staying at arm's length—but having enough of a relationship

that they had opportunities to confront situations without causing conflict. They had the authority to speak to the youngsters '
because of the consistency with which they lived by the same
rules of good conduct they were promoting.

Model respect for others. Keep in mind that the most
influential form of teaching is behavioral modeling. Practicing
your philosophy generates more respect than a good argument. If each of us just modeled a respect-giving life, much of
the training of younger generations would be accomplished
without extensive programming. Much as the Jews of Jesus'
day taught values to their children through their personal
lifestyle choices and family dialogue about those decisions,
so, too, could Americans pass along the fundamentals of
respectful living. In San Quentin, the Lifers modeled respectful behavior to the short-timers in much the same way that the
apostle Paul encouraged the Philippians to mimic his behavior
and values so that they would have the peace of God in their
hearts (Philippians 3:17–4:9).

We can show respect to people in many ways:

- We can respect their space by not invading their privacy
  or territory.
- We can respect their relationships by avoiding gossip or
  destructive words about family or friends.
- We can respect their vocations by not putting down their
  job or their performance.
- We can respect their lifestyles by accepting their personal
  choices in music, clothing, hairstyles, and the like.

- We can respect their belongings by not stealing from them.
- We can respect their lives by refraining from physical attacks.

Imagine what the world would be like if such norms were followed. We would not have a thriving paparazzi and celebrity culture. The media wouldn't seek to constantly publicize the gaffes and idiosyncrasies of public figures. There would be no tolerance for ugly remarks about people's race, age, social standing, or personal taste. Instead, we would have a deeper appreciation for the fact that God made us to be different from each other, and we would see beauty rather than threat in those differences.

TRANSFORMING PRINCIPLE

To get respect, you first have to give it.

CHAPTER 11

Persevere until You "Get It"

Some days when I woke up on my flimsy mattress on the
uncomfortable top bunk in my tiny cell—with my head just
inches below the ceiling and a few inches from the toilet—
it took me a little while before I remembered where I was.
After a minute or two, the gears would start moving and I
would remember I was still in San Quentin, alive for another
day. Many days, that simple fact seemed more than I could
bear. But it happened day after miserable day. And somehow
I was able to keep going, despite my circumstances.

As I watched others around me also struggling to make
it through the pain of one more day in prison, I observed a
determined diligence within each of the Lifers, and I realized
I had no choice. I could not give up. Ever. Indeed, just thinking
about the fact that millions of people over the course of human
history had been in similar or worse states than I was in—and
had made it through—gave me a morsel of hope.

Prison taught me that I am a lot tougher and stronger

than I thought. That's not reflective of anything special about me; it's a statement about the untapped resilience of human beings. Nobody inside the walls of San Quentin walked in fear of me because of my imposing physical presence or menacing scowl, but even so, I *was* tough enough to eventually get on top of my circumstances and ride them out to a great conclusion. The principles I was learning from the Lifers were the key to that recovery. But for the journey to have a favorable ending, perseverance was one of the irreplaceable ingredients in the mix.

I have always loved movies. In college I minored in drama and participated in dramatic productions—not because I sensed that my life was destined to turn into one big soap opera after graduation, but because of my appreciation for the craft and talent that bring stories to life.

One movie that always struck a resonant note with me was *Angus*, a cute little story about a high school guy who is too scared to ask a certain girl to the prom. His grandfather tries to encourage him, telling him that all he needs is courage. From the teen's perspective, he might as well have been asked to concoct the cure for cancer. Glumly, he responds, "I'm not Superman."

The grandfather's response is brilliant. "Superman isn't brave. . . . He's smart, handsome, even decent. But he's not brave. . . . Superman is indestructible, and you can't be brave if you're indestructible."

Courage is not the absence of fear, it's the decision to move forward in spite of the fear. We all enjoy stories where the underdog defeats impossible odds. People around the world embraced Rocky Balboa, the working-class boxer who transcended the streets of Philadelphia to become the heavyweight champion of the world in the *Rocky* films. For many decades we have wept at the classic story of Jean Valjean, the petty criminal in *Les Misérables* who emerges as a man of noble character. Every Christmas, millions return to the story of George Bailey, the honest family man who overcomes debt, trickery, and despair in *It's a Wonderful Life*. People gain strength from the true-life tale of James Braddock, a washed-up boxer who kept his family going through the thin times in *Cinderella Man*. Even the story of Jesus Christ is a tale of someone rejected by society, misunderstood by His own followers, and ultimately murdered unjustly before rising again. These are the stories that inspire us to do what we imagined could not be done.

Perhaps we appreciate these tales because in some small way, we hope we might be able to experience something like them. The story of Angus is heartwarming, but during my early years in prison, it was obvious that I was no Superman: I was incarcerated because I lacked strength of character. My early days spent sobbing in the yard demonstrated my lack of courage. I remained in my own personal prison because I was not able to move beyond my fear.

But what I had not yet considered was that God did not intend for me to ultimately fail. He gave me life because He passionately wanted a vibrant relationship with me. And He had a great plan for my life. He allowed the struggles and the suffering to help me become the person He created me to be. He needed to prepare me for the life He had laid out for me.

We can take heart from the apostle Paul's adventures. His résumé was stellar. He started out in glorious fashion: a star pupil of the leading Jewish scholars, a prodigy among the Pharisees, a renowned teacher and debater. But then he met God, and everything changed. This God, who supposedly loved him so much, allowed Paul's life to be ruined beyond recognition. In Paul's own words:

> I have worked much harder, been in prison more frequently, been flogged more severely, and been exposed to death again and again. Five times I received from the Jews the forty lashes minus one. Three times I was beaten with rods, once I was stoned, three times I was shipwrecked, I spent a night and a day in the open sea, I have been constantly on the move. I have been in danger from rivers, in danger from bandits, in danger from my own countrymen, in danger from Gentiles; in danger in the city, in danger in the country, in danger at sea; and in danger from false brothers. I have labored and toiled and have often gone without sleep; I have known hunger and thirst and have often gone without food; I have been cold and naked. (2 Corinthians 11:23-27)

Clearly, Paul was no stranger to hardship and pain. From my perspective, he had every reason—every right—to turn his back on God and return to a less dangerous way of life. But he didn't. Paul explained that we are capable of handling the trials and temptations we encounter because God—the same God who allowed Paul to undergo all those horrendous experiences—is faithful to us and will show us the path to endurance and triumph. This was all part of God's best plan for Paul—maybe not the easiest plan, but definitely the best plan. And Paul knew it.

I read this passage in my cell and in the prison chapel over and over. Although it was encouraging, it didn't make my trials any easier to withstand. Persevering through tough times wears a person down; the ordeal can seem overwhelming. We do not have control of our lives or environment. We are at the mercy of forces that dictate our circumstances. We're not helpless, but neither are we able to call the shots at will. More often than not, we have to roll with the punches. Sometimes, as in my case, the punches don't feel as if they are ever going to let up.

I understand the pressure to give up. When I arrived inside those walls at San Quentin, I felt a death sentence upon my heart. It was clear to me that nothing good could come out of this ordeal, and in my mind there was a better-than-average possibility that I would never emerge from that forsaken place. The pain and pressure were relentless; every moment of every day I was immersed in the certainty that I was a doomed man and that my life would never be reclaimed and restored. This wasn't pretend Hollywood pain; this was the real deal. It hurt so much, for so long, that I became numb to everything except my pain.

How quickly things can change. In Oakland, I was the boy wonder. In San Quentin, I was the boy whiner.

It's hard to keep going when you feel as if the world has you in a choke hold. It's tough to fight back when you're out of strength and there's no one in your corner to urge you on. It's discouraging when each effort you make seems to drag you down further. It's depressing to know that, even in the best of circumstances, you will be a captive for years to come. It's exhausting to continually present your case to deaf ears. It's demoralizing to realize that your situation is the natural consequence of your ill-advised behavior.

Early in the fight, I was on the verge of giving up. Thankfully, I didn't.

One reason I made it through was that I had just enough faith in God—barely enough—to trust that there must be some purpose for my suffering and some way through it. My faith was probably no more than the size of the proverbial mustard seed, but as the Bible teaches, that was sufficient. I realized that I had no choice but to reach out to God, even though I could not see Him or feel Him. For isn't that what faith is all about?

And even though I couldn't yet see Him, God gave me the strength and ability I needed to take that first step toward wholeness. The only thing I had to do was choose to act.

Sure enough, as time passed, it dawned on me that this entire San Quentin experience was designed to do something special in my life, through the shaping of my character. The story of Job took on a whole new meaning to me; I could relate to his suffering in ways that an academic reading of his tale could never convey. Job is an incredible tale of suffering and abandonment. But he was pulled through it by God, who then blessed him with about twice as much in the second half of his life.

Another thing that kept me going was the nagging sense that if I completely gave up I would miss out on something special that was meant to happen in my life. I wholeheartedly believed David's declaration of faith in Psalm 27:13-14: "I am still confident of this: I will see the goodness of the Lord *in the land of the living.* Wait for the Lord; be strong and take heart and wait for the Lord" (italics added). Ah, it was the "wait" part that was so painful.

Yes, I had times when I was so mentally and spiritually weak that I was just taking up space, not really fighting for my life. But the Lord kept me going, and eventually I eased out of my tailspin. Amazingly, even when I was curled in a ball in the yard, I still had a distant, vague sense that my life had a purpose and that my purpose had not yet been revealed or realized. I had only the faintest of hopes that perhaps there was something very good and special yet to come. But it was hope, even if it was simply based on curiosity.

At one point in my ordeal, it occurred to me that after I died I would have to face God. In my rudimentary understanding of the faith at that point, I assumed He would review my life with me and then show me what He had planned for my future. His words through Jeremiah the prophet haunted me: "'For I know the plans I have for you,' declares the LORD, 'plans to prosper you and not to harm you, plans to give you hope and a future. Then you will call upon me and come and pray to me, and I will listen to you'" (Jeremiah 29:11-12). I was convinced I had not yet experienced the good portion of those plans, certainly not the hopeful future that was alluded to. So I assumed there was more to come. It had to be better than what I had experienced so far—and that seemed worth sticking around for. I did not want to miss out on whatever great stuff the Lord had in store for me.

Another motivation not to give up was the realization that, despite all of my problems and disappointments, somehow I kept going. When the business collapsed, I thought that was the end of my life. But my life kept going. When the courts handed down the sentence that consigned me to the corrections system, I figured that was the final straw. But my life kept going. When I set foot in the first prison where I was to learn the ropes and then be reassigned, there was no doubt in my mind that my life was worthless and would soon end. But my life kept going. When I had to urinate in my small cell with my cellie's head just a couple of feet away and take a shower in a confined space with dozens of other naked felons while armed guards watched, I could not imagine a more embarrassing or degrading moment. But my life kept going. Simply setting foot inside San Quentin convinced me that my life was done. But my life kept going. The worst day of my life—when everything went dark and hopeless—was surely the beginning of the end. But I still woke up every morning, and my life kept going.

Somehow, each new experience pulled me lower and lower until finally I was sure I had bottomed out. But, to my amazement, life continued and I was able to keep going. I realized that I was more resilient than I had imagined, and with that in mind, I decided it was time to take a really big leap of faith.

Although I was beginning to overcome much of the anxiety and depression I had suffered when first entering San Quentin, I still struggled in a number of other ways. I had developed a pretty severe case of obsessive-compulsive disorder—washing my hands twenty to thirty times a day, hoarding books and magazines, obsessing over everything. I knew these actions were simply symptoms of a bigger problem, but I felt powerless to stop them. Finally one day, I looked back over all that I had been through and knew it was time to make a choice. I could continue to allow my compulsions to control me, or I could put my trust in God.

I chose God. I quit the OCD behaviors cold turkey. It was the biggest step of faith that I had ever taken up to that point. And I was okay. Nothing bad happened to me when I stopped washing my hands. Life simply went on—and I survived.

Humans are much more durable than we sometimes believe. We are mesmerized by the stories of people like Don Piper, the pastor who survived a physically debilitating car accident and, after dying and spending ninety minutes in heaven, recovered and launched a productive ministry. The diving accident that crippled Joni Eareckson Tada led to a worldwide ministry that advocates for those with disabilities and provides inspiration to millions of people. Nick Vujicic was born without arms and legs but has learned to overcome his physical limitations and speaks words of encouragement to hundreds of thousands of people worldwide, moving them to focus on the opportunities rather than the obstacles. The list of people who have survived amazing circumstances and now lead productive lives is robust. People survive accidents, diseases, divorces, the loss of loved ones, financial disasters, natural disasters, and so much more.

III

Maybe your life doesn't have anything quite as dramatic as a prison term, a near-fatal car accident, or a debilitating physical handicap. Even so, you still might feel as if you cannot handle what the world has thrown at you. Welcome to the club. As my friend Phyllis Hendry says, "The most difficult thing about life is that it's daily." The challenges are part of life—a part that we can endure if we are committed to doing so and willing to rely upon the strength that God provides, even when we don't necessarily feel it. We all go through dark times. But if inmates locked in tiny cells behind huge prison walls can muster the will and energy to overcome their darkest hours, so can you.

I'd like to tell you that I found the secret to endurance, that there are five can't-miss steps to perseverance. I can't. Somehow, I made it through. So did my Lifer buddies. There is no magic formula. But some of the actions that helped us can help you make it through too.

When the tough times strike, start your defense by recognizing and accepting your God-given ability to persevere. That is not easy. When we face giants, we focus on the giants, not the slingshot and the stones in our pockets. But your ability to triumph begins with the mental certainty that you have what it takes to overcome your obstacles. This is not because of anything you have done; it is because God made you strong and resilient. He wants to shape you, not destroy you. Many of His great followers—Job, Abraham, Joseph, Moses, David, Solomon, Isaiah, Jeremiah, John the Baptist, John, Peter, and Paul—experienced hardship as a way of life for a season and a reason. In every case, God used the difficulties in meaningful ways. As Joseph told his brothers, who had thrown him in a pit and sold him into slavery, "You intended to harm me, but God intended it for good to accomplish what is now being done, the saving of many lives" (Genesis 50:20). Indeed, some of the best examples of leadership come from those times when people were under the greatest strain and stress.

Never give up. You were made to make it through the darkness. To quote Friedrich Nietzsche, what doesn't kill you makes you stronger.

As you navigate the rapids of suffering, cling to God's promises. The Bible is packed with references to how He will respond to your distress. The Psalms are a string of heartfelt cries from David to God, followed by God's reassurance that He will do what is right. God's promise to Jacob is the same promise He made—and kept—with me, and He will do the same for you. "I will not leave you until I have done what I have promised you" (Genesis 28:15). The Lord promises that although we will face trials and tribulations, if we stay focused on Him, He will carry us through the pain—no matter how long it takes (see John 16:33; Hebrews 13:5-6).

Like a soldier in the battle zone, stockpile the weapons you will need in your fight for survival and victory. As Jesus told His followers, much to their confusion, our weapons are not guns and swords, or even political power and authority. We win this battle through the power of God, received in response to our constant and faithful prayers and sometimes not-so-faithful prayers. So often we dismiss prayer as well-intentioned but powerless words spoken into the air. But our God, who sees and hears everything, gets excited when we demonstrate our faith and trust in Him by expressing our needs in prayer.

Honestly, there were days—sometimes weeks—in San Quentin when I barely had the strength to breathe, much less muster an articulate prayer to God. And He understands that weakness. That's part of the process of being broken of our arrogance and self-reliance so that we lean totally on Him. And if you don't have the strength or clarity of mind to even know what to pray for, or how to pray, He has provided the solution for that too. He gives us the Holy Spirit to represent us before His throne. You don't have to explain to God the outcome that's needed, or even the strategy by which He can achieve that outcome for you. You simply need to trust God's wisdom and power, and let Him figure it out. As He promises, the Holy Spirit will intercede on your behalf so that you can receive the things only God understands and is able to grant (Romans 8:26-28).

Early on in my struggle, things deteriorated because I insisted that I was the key player in my situation. How wrong I was! Later on I learned that this thinking is as common as it is destructive. Vy Le was mired in his anger and agony in the Hole until it dawned on him that the solution to his crisis was beyond his capabilities. In fact, every one of the Lifers I looked up to for guidance eventually arrived at that same conclusion: We cannot fight the good fight on our own. It is a fight of faith—faith in the God who reminds us, "The LORD will fight for you; you need only to be still" (Exodus 14:14).

Borrow strength from family and friends. If they love you, you bless them by allowing them to help you, and their help will be a blessing in return. Again, my struggle to get through the darkness would never have progressed had it not been for the tangible help given by people who cared about me. For me, relying on others for strength was not a concept I understood, much less accepted. Fortunately, God orchestrated my recovery in such a way that my pride did not block the blessing He had in store.

My parents came to visit me every Saturday in San Quentin, and over time, I began to really look forward to their visits—not so much because of what they could *do* for me, but just because I liked being with them. Only then was I able to actually draw true strength from that relationship.

But as much as I enjoyed those Saturday morning visits with my mom and stepdad, I found that as our time together was winding down, I was just as excited to return back to the yard, back to the Lifers. These guys had become my lifeline, and I couldn't wait to be back in their presence—so much so that I didn't even mind the mandatory strip search I had to endure before being allowed back into the yard.

One of the greatest ways the Lifers helped me was simply by allowing me inside their world so I could discover how they broke through their pain to wholeness. When someone experienced that breakthrough, we'd say, "He gets it." Reaching that new level released that person to make strides toward wellness and wholeness. Talking to Vy, Binh, Michael, Sam, Kevin, and others gave me a window into their pain and triumph. They served as models of hope merely by discussing the highs and lows of their journeys. My return to vitality was built on the backs of these men.

Set manageable, achievable daily goals. As you try to get through each day, stay focused on these small goals. The more you can keep your eyes off your problems and concentrate on accomplishing a simple task, the more your pain will ease and you will begin to regain some self-confidence. It's a slow process, but everything good takes time to develop.

I had gained about thirty pounds since arriving in San Quentin—the result of a starch-heavy diet, very little physical exercise, and a deep depression. I decided it was time to lose some weight. I wasn't trying to impress anyone—I was in prison; who was I going to impress? I simply wanted to feel better and have something positive to work toward.

I made a conscious effort to eat less and make better

choices. I began to work out in the weight yard with all the big guys. And every day, I walked the perimeter of the yard, transferring rocks from one pocket to another to help me keep track of the number of laps I completed. Eventually, I achieved my goal and lost all of the extra weight. In fact, I was in the best shape I had ever been. The sense of accomplishment I felt was amazing, and this helped me overcome my depression.

Each day, as you finish the job you set out to do, celebrate that success. Unless you encourage yourself by seeing and acknowledging forward movement, your motivation to keep setting goals and moving ahead will wane. Give yourself permission to recognize your achievement. God doesn't make losers.

If you're like me, sometimes you read passages in the Bible that don't seem to penetrate your consciousness; ten seconds after reading them you cannot recall what you read. Other times, you read a passage that freezes you in place because it so captures or speaks to your situation that it seems as if God wrote those words just for that moment, just for you. Chills run through your body. I experienced that with this passage:

> Not only so, but we also rejoice in our sufferings,
> because we know that suffering produces persever-
> ance; perseverance, character; and character, hope.
> And hope does not disappoint us, because God
> has poured out his love into our hearts by the Holy
> Spirit, whom he has given us. (Romans 5:3-5)

In a nutshell, that's the story of my life. Unlimited potential, squandered through stupidity and selfishness, resulting in brokenness; perseverance facilitating the rebuilding of my character, the recovery of hope, and the joy of life restored. What a strange but glorious journey it has been. Without the determination to endure beyond my own strength, it could not have happened.

TRANSFORMING PRINCIPLE
Never give up. Ever. Persevere until you "get it."

CHAPTER 12

Let Life Come to You

One of the best things the Lifers taught me was to throw out the calendar I had in my cell. My tendency was to keep looking at it longingly, calculating how much more time I had until I'd be eligible for parole. It was agonizing to realize how slowly the time passed—especially when I kept looking at the calendar, waiting for yet another day to expire.

One day, I realized the Lifers didn't have calendars in their cells. This made sense to me. What good would it do? A calendar was just a bitter reminder of all the days we had lost because of our own foolishness. The only thing we could count on for certain was the current moment. So rather than focusing on the past or the future, we needed to get the most out of the present.

The larger lesson God was trying to teach me was the importance of letting life come to me, rather than trying to retain control over everything around me. The issues that sent me to prison were a result of my insistence on determining every detail of everything I laid my hands on. It was time to learn an alternative strategy for life.

Letting go, however, was no easy task. One of the prison counselors I met with during my stay recognized my dilemma and gave me some advice. "You're trying to do your entire twelve hundred days every single day. Just focus on today." He encouraged me to let go of the reins of my world and allow God to orchestrate my steps. He was not a Christian, but he was nudging me toward a firsthand understanding of Jesus' recommendation: "Do not worry about tomorrow, for tomorrow will worry about itself. Each day has enough trouble of its own" (Matthew 6:34).

Once I understood the importance of releasing my iron grip on life's controls, I began to notice that inmates handled their time in one of three ways. The first group included people who were blown away by being imprisoned—as I had been. The reality of life behind bars was so overwhelming that they became comatose. They shuffled through the day, eyes glazed, doing what they were told without any hint of objection or resistance and without any trace of mental or emotional investment in the process. They were almost robotic. Sadly, these inmates lacked purpose and direction. A significant share of the inmates in this segment were mentally ill and had no capacity to respond more meaningfully, either because of the severity of their illnesses or the dulling effects of their medications. Those who were not mentally ill but who responded this way were just as sad to behold.

A second group was made up of those who resisted surrendering control to the prison system. As they tried to remain masters of their own destinies, you could almost hear these convicts shouting "You won't break me" at the CO who was writing them up for yet another prison fight or putting them in lockdown for more bad behavior. Unfortunately, however, the only thing they really accomplished was adding more time to their sentence or prolonging the time until they might be seriously considered for parole. Their anger and self-reliance kept them alert and energized, but it also prevented them from making progress toward recovery.

Of course, the most outrageous examples are those men who tried to escape from prison. These were among the favorite tales told in prison (think campfire stories). Many of the short-timers listened carefully to these narratives, seeking some clues that might help them dream up their own escape plan. The Lifers, however, related these stories with glee, laughing at the stupidity of the efforts and the inability of the people involved to realize that none of us can force life to conform to our will.

My personal favorite was about a guy who had probably watched too many old prison movies and thought he'd outsmart the system by mimicking what had worked on the big screen. This fellow tracked the movement of the laundry truck inside San Quentin day after day, figuring out the time patterns, the personnel involved, the security routine, and other details that would be integral to his escape plan. He figured he would hide in one of the laundry bins before it was loaded onto the truck and then leap to freedom after it left the grounds.

Finally the day arrived for this guy to pull the trigger on his plan. Sneaking into a truck, he dove into one of the large laundry carts and expertly hid himself, just like in the movies. The back door of the truck rolled down, and the truck rumbled to life and took off. The inmate could almost taste his freedom as he prepared to jump from the back of the moving truck.

This enterprising young man had overlooked just one small detail: the laundry truck never went outside the walls of San Quentin. It drove from cell block to cell block, and building to building, picking up laundry as it made its way to the far end of the complex where the laundry facilities were housed.

That is the tale of a guy who had no idea how to let life come to him! And, of course, his escape attempt simply prolonged his sentence—and made him the laughingstock of the prison for years to come.

The final group of prisoners was made up of people who accepted their situation for what it was—unfortunate but unalterable. Accepting their circumstances—which they had instigated—they decided to make the best of the situation and use their experiences as a means to growth. Some prisoners entered the walls with that mentality already in place, but more often this was a perspective that inmates embraced only after they spent some time in the system, having gained some distance from the world's distractions and distortions. Once they could think more clearly and strategically, they learned a significant lesson about life: we cannot control the world, so we must let it come to us. When it does, we can choose how to respond most appropriately.

The earliest illustration I had of this principle was

provided by my friend Vy Le. After many years and struggles, Vy had become one of the most popular and trusted prisoners in San Quentin. The guards knew and appreciated him. His employers within the prison liked his work ethic, honesty, and upbeat attitude. Other inmates accepted him as a beacon of hope for their own transformation. Gone were the days when Vy was angry with everyone and everything. He had arrived at a place of peace in his mind and heart; he had reached a state in which he either had to trust God to orchestrate the best outcome for his circumstances or admit that his God was powerless and his faith in that God was worthless. He chose to believe that God was in control.

Because of his widespread acceptance by the administration and inmates alike and because his prison job required him to travel all over the San Quentin compound, Vy had an ID card that gave him broad access. But for reasons unknown to us, on some days the guards would refuse to give him access to certain parts of the grounds, no matter how important his errand or assigned task. I never saw him question or complain about those interruptions to his schedule; he would simply turn around and, with a smile on his face, return to the place from which he had come.

On other days, he would have to go to a part of the prison that was protected by heavy security. That necessitated waiting, sometimes for long periods, while a door was unlocked or other security measures were performed. Vy always waited patiently, without demonstrating irritation or displeasure over the delay.

Sometimes, as he walked from his office to another area,

a new guard would be at a checkpoint and rather than just wave Vy through, as was the custom, the guard would hold him up and check his badge thoroughly before allowing him to continue. Vy never got upset about those holdups or the slight of not being known or trusted. He understood that it was part of a process he could not control or change. He accepted it for what it was: an insignificant hiccup in a larger portfolio of experiences that day.

It was as though Vy had internalized the words of the Serenity Prayer: "God, grant me the serenity to accept the things I cannot change; courage to change the things I can; and wisdom to know the difference."

III

How are you doing with this? When plans are disrupted, does it throw you for a loop? When things don't go your way, does it ruin your day, or do you accept it as a minor disruption? Do you let life come to you, or do you try to force the outcome? In essence, the Lifers had their entire lives disrupted, and yet they refused to allow petty irritations over the course of a single day to ruin their positive outlooks.

I am an avid sports fan, and I have watched in fascination as some of the great coaches in professional sports employ this principle of letting life come to you. Joe Torre, the great baseball manager, quietly and respectfully dispenses fatherly advice or encouragement to his players when needed. He remains calm in the midst of turmoil, but he deals with conditions as they arise, demonstrating patience, wisdom, and focus. Tony Dungy, who has led various pro football teams to great success, deals with the stresses and strains of life on the sidelines, as well as in his personal life, with great composure and dignity. He is known to be a competent leader of men, moving them forward with quiet strength, passion, and godly character. These are two of the most respected coaches within the last decade. Yes, they are both winning coaches, but is that why we respect them? No. They are most admired for their ability to remain calm in the midst of life's turmoil and storms.

Making the transition from a type A, make-it-happen kind of guy to someone who voluntarily gives the reins of his life to God has not been a simple transition for me. The first hurdle was realizing that letting life come to me was not the same as giving up and becoming a victim. If you're used to visualizing a future and calling the shots to bring that vision to reality, taking a step back to allow God to dictate the future seems like an admission of failure, a weakness, or a recipe for disaster. Ironically, allowing God to arrange life is not the same as rolling over to become a victim, whereas steadfastly holding on to control is more likely to turn you into one.

The trick is to pull your weight in pursuing the things that matter without forcing the outcomes. Achieving the proper balance is very difficult at first. But you can only do what you can do, and after a while it becomes a more natural practice. Like anything, balance does become a habit, but it takes time and repetition for it to become ingrained.

At first I found it difficult to release my past and stop

worrying about the future. I had heard sermons and other encouragement about relying upon God, and at some level, I knew that my stubborn refusal to surrender control was only blocking Him from doing what was best for me. A lot of my resistance was driven by fear about what would happen if I did not press forward to create a better future for myself. I firmly believed that God was all-knowing and all-powerful, but I did not see how that translated into His crafting a realistic, day-to-day plan for my future.

But one day I encountered a memorable, mind-shifting message. I don't remember where I first saw it, but it was significant enough that I wrote it in the margin of my Bible. Apparently it had appeared on a Hallmark greeting card in the seventies. It was written by someone who seemed to be struggling with the exact issue I was daunted by: paralysis related to the past and future. The text, written by Helen Mallicoat, went like this:

> *I was regretting the past and fearing the future. Suddenly my Lord was speaking: "My name is I AM." He paused. I waited.*
>
> *He continued, "When you live in the past with its mistakes and regrets, it is hard. I AM not there. My name is not I WAS.*
>
> *"When you live in the future, with its problems and fears, it is hard. I AM not there. My name is not I WILL BE.*
>
> *"When you live in the moment, it is not hard. I AM here. My name is I AM."*

Ultimately, then, my choice is simple: Do I want to live in the past, where God no longer is? Do I want to live in the future, where God is not yet? Or do I want to live in the present, fully experiencing the gift of this moment He has granted me and wants to guide me through? It's a no-brainer.

But even a no-brainer takes some brains when it comes to figuring out the "how to." This has been an evolving process for me. But here are the things I've learned about letting life come to me, rather than trying to make it what I think it should be.

Really trust God. We talk all the time about how important it is to trust God, and we try to offer evidence that shows just how much we trust Him. But if we're being honest, it doesn't seem that we trust God as much as we want ourselves and others to believe. We often feel as if we have to help Him produce the outcomes we desire.

The peace that some Lifers had after being turned down for parole time after time gave me a firsthand glimpse at what trusting God looks like. You have to have a viable reason to sustain hope; in prison, parole was such a reason. To have that longing consistently dashed was emotionally devastating. But my friends had incredible faith that God knew what was best. "Yes, I want to get out very much, but when the time is right, God will bring my parole through," was Vy's response. He had not given up hope; he simply had given up trying to will his way out of prison.

For me, the first step to really trusting God has been to fully own the notion that He cares enough to exert control over my life; that He loves me enough to be intimately involved in all the details of my existence; and that He is wise enough to make better decisions than I would.

In practical terms, that means accepting His timing and allowing Him to use unexpected people and events to make a big difference in my life. If He truly knows what's best, loves me as much as the Bible claims, and has the capacity to do what's best for me, then I have to let go and let God do His thing on my behalf. After all, I took matters into my own hands and messed up pretty badly; that's what got me into prison in the first place. God couldn't do much worse, and there's ample evidence that He can and does do things much better.

Accept the natural pace and flow of life. Many of us— especially the type As—need the adrenaline rush of the next deal, the quick production schedule, the bigger product, the more dramatic plan, or whatever it is that suggests we are making significant things happen. Even when we are able to generate the outcomes we envision, we often cannot enjoy the fruits of our labor because of the stress we place ourselves under or the excessive price we have to pay to facilitate those outcomes (such as broken marriages, poor relationships with our children, fractured friendships, illness, legal entanglements, etc.).

I now understand that I allowed the rush of activity to propel me because I was viewing the world through my lenses, not God's. He doesn't need anything that I produce in order for His will and His world to operate smoothly and effectively. Once I get in line with His agenda rather than mine and let

Him determine the pace and flow of my life in concert with His purposes, everything seems to stabilize.

Take time to enjoy the ride. God wants to provide us with a meaningful journey—not without some challenges along the way, but an adventure that is packed with excitement and revelation. It's all too easy to get so wound up in productivity and other self-determined challenges that we miss the fun and beauty of the life He designed just for us. For me, grasping the pleasure of the experience has been a learned skill; in fact, it's one that I'm still perfecting. Enjoying our days on earth is meant to be part of the blessing of the gift of life.

Observe God at work in other people's lives. God often uses the lives of others to help us understand how He works and what He is already doing in our lives. Sometimes when watching the foolishness of others, I realize we cause our own hardships. Sometimes I see how God comes through in the clutch for people who don't deserve such favor, and I realize He's done the same for me. In all of those experiences, God is showing me how He works in everyone's life, including mine, even though my own spiritual blindness keeps me from noticing all of His handiwork. People's lives can be a mirror to our own experiences.

Eliminate petty jealousy. Yes, sometimes I still look at other people's success and feel a twinge of envy. *I could have done that—even better*, I've thought more than a couple of times in the past few years while watching or reading about someone's business victories. But my emotion is drawing me away from the point: I have an opportunity to learn from the other person's journey and to celebrate the glorious thing God has done in his or her life. Someone else's success never robs me of the opportunity to become all He has in store for me. Only I can lose that opportunity through my unchecked emotions or inappropriate responses. Those who find joy in the victories of others—this was something I learned from the Lifers—lose no sleep over their own lack of supremacy or accomplishment. They appreciate that God rules all of us, that everyone is different and has a unique calling, and that those who work with God get to see the Master Craftsman weaving it all together in an incredible display of authority and creativity.

One of the finest examples of this largehearted nature was exhibited by Jason. A Lifer who has been in prison for more than twenty years, Jason took the job of training short-timers on how to reenter society successfully. He instructed them in things like applying for a driver's license, opening a bank account, getting health insurance, obtaining bus passes, and the like—basic tasks that they would have to master to get them through each day.

Here was a guy who might never get outside the walls again, devoting himself to preparing these younger criminals to succeed. Think about the kind of heart that takes. There was no shred of envy in him; he kept that job even though other positions were available. Jason was always thrilled on the rare occasions when he heard back from one of his former students whose life was going well. The sole benefit he received from the job was the knowledge that he was equipping those men to transition smoothly back into a world that was generally unsympathetic to their plight. Jason had the kind of heart that enabled those men to let life come to them, in whatever form or fashion God chose.

Observe, reflect, appreciate. There are no accidents in life; everything happens for a reason. Every individual has a God-given purpose within the pursuit of His plan for humanity. If all of these notions are true—and I believe they are—then every life experience is simply an opportunity to learn something that will help me be the man God made me to be. Learning requires me to analyze and reflect upon what is going on around me and to grasp how God intends that experience to shape and help me.

Grow all the time. I once heard a pastor say that if you aren't growing, you're dying—there is no in-between condition. Sometimes we get in a rut, become comfortable, and don't grow. When we enter that vegetative state, God can't do much with us. I've noticed that when I get lazy—intellectually, spiritually, emotionally, or physically—I don't see what God is doing or how I can best respond to the new opportunities He is opening for me. One way to make sure you're always growing is to conduct a daily inventory before going to bed, listing what you saw or learned that day that pushed you to be closer to the person God created you to be. If you can't identify anything specific, that's a warning that you may be getting complacent and need to push yourself to plow some new ground. If you *can* specify something learned or discovered that day, try to incorporate it into the nucleus of who you are—the new person God is continually enabling you to become.

Do everything with integrity. If we want life to come to us as God wills, then we must be sure to respond to everything with integrity. Our words must be true. Our emotions must be honest. We cannot manipulate people in order to get our own way. Our motives must be pure. We should be transparent and vulnerable, trusting God to protect and guide us. The old computer acronym *WYSIWYG*, which stands for "what you see is what you get," should be an accurate description of our lives, and that description should be one that always honors God. Otherwise, chances are good that we are simply playing games to get our own way and twisting life for our own dubious purposes.

You may think you don't need integrity, and that it will all work out in the end. You may believe that the ends justify the means. But you're only fooling yourself. I tried that, and trust me, it didn't go well.

It's important to remember that the Christian life is a process of growing to become more like Jesus. There are days when I probably have only the faintest resemblance to Jesus, but the more I can train myself to stay true to the principles I learned in San Quentin that conform to the teachings of God's Word, the better my life becomes.

TRANSFORMING PRINCIPLE
Let life come to you rather than trying to retain control over everything.

CHAPTER 13

Make Life Simple

In the world outside of San Quentin, twenty-four hours never seems to be enough time to get everything done that we want to accomplish or experience, so we are constantly looking for ways to stretch or multiply time. But inside the walls, the idea was just the opposite: to slow the day down to a crawl so that inmates could mentally and emotionally process their pasts and their futures more clearly.

A life in slow motion enabled those of us who had suffered from a lack of contemplation to come face-to-face with who we were, who we wanted to be, who we could be, what we had done, what we could have done, and what we would do. Those are questions I should have addressed more thoughtfully before prison but instead had pushed out of my mind in the whirlwind of activity that filled my days. The consequence was that I made decisions on the run, relying on mental and emotional reflexes to guide me. While not every decision based on reflex reactions results in a criminal offense, I discovered that it's unwise to live at a breakneck pace, relying so heavily on instinct.

You may be familiar with the saying, "If you're not stressed out and overscheduled, you're not alive." That seems like a pretty good summary of life these days. But my life is proof that it's also a pretty good way of getting in trouble.

During my boy wonder years, time was a precious commodity. There were never enough hours in a day. In the fast lane, it was imperative to own all the latest stuff, know the right people, and be seen at the most prestigious parties. My workdays were long, and if there was any time left at the end of a day, I could always find plenty of people who needed no excuse to let off steam in nightclubs and private celebrations.

To say that my life was cluttered would be a gross understatement. In retrospect, I can see that the unyielding pace and scale of activity in my life severely challenged any hope I had of being a man of integrity. If nothing else, the sheer velocity at which my life moved left no time for reflection about the methods, motives, and implications of my choices. This pedal-to-the-metal lifestyle contributed mightily to my downfall and imprisonment. Busyness and complexity made me feel like I was really accomplishing something special. In reality, I confused busyness with significance. That mistake undermined the foundations of my life.

Prisons are designed to "reprogram" inmates—that is, to change their thinking in the hope that it will lead to changed behavior. Part of that reprogramming includes giving inmates

a less jumbled and disorienting life, largely by offering fewer
options and by helping them establish stable routines and
habits. One of the crucial assumptions underlying prisoner
rehabilitation is that inmates made bad choices because they
did not properly analyze the validity and implications of their
options. The antidote, then, was to place them in an artificial
environment that offered fewer options, more time for reflection, and guidance in decision making.

When I was placed in San Quentin, one of the most
refreshing realities was that the pace of life inside the walls
was slow. Not that I was in any shape to notice or appreciate
that at first: I was still so obsessed with the misery of my situation that everything happening around me was just white
noise. It took months before my mind and body rhythms
slowed down to correspond to the intentionally deliberate
pace of the prison life.

Once I became aware of how the speed and complexity
of my life context had been altered, though, I was positively
impacted by the change of pace. Not only was life sluggish,
but the prison minimized external distractions and presented
fewer choices for me to make. What a relief! Outside the walls,
I would have considered the pace and routine of San Quentin
to be absurdly slow and mind-numbing. Inside the walls,
however, I derived a certain stability and comfort from our
decelerated existence. It was definitely a contrived environment, but one with merit.

Some inmates entered prison addicted to drugs or alcohol, but almost all of us entered as addicts to the fast-moving,

materialistic, me-first life. Until I was detoxed of that addiction, I didn't realize that much of what I had once considered necessary for survival or success was really just unnecessary "stuff." Prison forced me to go cold turkey in order to cleanse my system from the obsessions that had been destroying me.

Contrary to popular thought—or at least my preprison thinking—healthy, comfortable survival actually requires very little. For instance, there was no Starbucks inside San Quentin. At one point, that was a horrifying thought to me, but I learned to get by with instant Folgers, which I happily drink to this day. Before entering prison, the hotels I stayed in on my business trips always had multiple pillows on each bed. In my cell, we were not allowed to have pillows, so I learned to do without. In my partying days as one of the rare white guys who enjoyed dancing, I always knew the latest dance-club tunes. Without a source of current music while behind bars, I lost touch with the pop-music scene—and yet life kept going. After the system had restructured my existence, I was astonished to discover how little I really required to live a contented, if seemingly Spartan, life.

I learned to find contentment in the simple things, and as a result, I experienced a feeling of peace that was beyond my comprehension. Some evenings, returning early from the yard, I would have to wait to be let into my cell. During that lull, I often strolled along the bottom tier that housed the Lifers and peeked in on the residents. What I observed was amazing. These men had virtually nothing inside their tiny homes, yet they had everything they needed to feel at peace—with

God, themselves, and the world. As I peered through the bars, I saw them writing, reading, watching the small TVs that were allowed in their cells, doing simple things that brought them pleasure.

From the tiers above I could hear the arguing and noisy rumblings from the short-timers. I knew that life within those short-timer cell blocks was anything but peaceful. But that agitation was unable to puncture the air of calm that enveloped the Lifers' floor. As another day neared its close, a blanket of tranquillity seemed to cover those tiers—a serene acceptance of the way things were.

III

Our frenetic pace puts us all at risk to differing degrees. Anxiety levels have risen through the roof: more than seventy million U.S. adults presently say they are "stressed out." Nearly half of the public admits to being "too busy." Three out of ten go so far as to say that life is getting too complicated to understand these days. And our culture doesn't offer much hope of improvement in this regard: half of all adults believe their lives are becoming more stressful with each passing year.[5]

In every dimension of life, Americans now expect to have a multitude of options available. This is even noticeable on grocery-store shelves (how many varieties of cereal or shampoo are possible—or necessary?). It is evident by the number of television channels and radio stations. Niche marketing has become the norm, with companies producing ever-more targeted products and services for a growing contingent of market segments.

Not even the religious world is immune to this trend. There are thousands of different English-language versions, translations, paraphrases, and editions of the Bible available. And churches offer all kinds of different worship styles to meet people's musical tastes and teaching preferences.

The frantic pace of life is seen in our felt need to have as many experiences and interactions as possible. That has made multitasking the rule of the day. People make phone calls while driving to the next appointment. People text while watching movies or eating meals. Kids do their homework with their iPod earbuds in place, the television on, and their computers fired up, texting all along. We are determined to squeeze every last opportunity from each moment.

Few of us are willing to cut back. It is the rare person who is willing to sacrifice the adrenaline rush in order to lead a simpler life. Most amazing of all is the fact that a huge majority of us are in denial regarding the effect this is having on our lives. Eighty-two percent of American adults claim they already lead a simple life. Huh? With record-setting levels of consumer debt and prescriptions for stress-relieving drugs, half of all new marriages ending in divorce, people getting less sleep than ever (and less than their bodies physically require), and people generally feeling overloaded by information and responsibilities, it's hard to imagine what it is about our lives that qualifies as simple.[6]

Thankfully, my frenetic-energy detox in San Quentin enabled me to become a quiet advocate for simplicity. I've come to see that taking time to read the Bible daily and to pray reflectively is a gift. Turning off the cell phone when you're in the car with your kids or putting aside the unread reports in order to have a meaningful conversation is priceless. Spending a few moments here and there to bask in the sunshine, to take pleasure in a quiet evening at home, or to appreciate the splendor of the mountainside is a treasure. Getting a good night of sleep, without worrying about waking early to get in an extra hour of work, is a joy.

Yet I'm reticent to become a more vocal supporter of living simply because I know how difficult it is to maintain such a lifestyle. Jesus prayed that His followers would be in the world but not of it, but I have found that a hard command to follow. This world equates simplicity to failure, irrelevance, boredom, or even ignorance. An addiction to adrenaline is tough to defeat. Expectations, opportunities, competition—it all adds up to a compelling invitation to ramp it up.

Ironically, the problem with living simply is that it's so complicated.

Think about those words: *It's complicated to live a simple life.*

So what did San Quentin teach me about the simple life? Perhaps it has to begin with a way of thinking. We believe that we can control our lives and produce better outcomes if we have more options from which to choose. Our view is that the greater the number of accessible alternatives we have, the better off we will be. But being ripped from the cultural environment long enough to get that perspective out of my system showed me the fallacy of such "more is better" thinking.

You don't have to spend time incarcerated to arrive at this conclusion. When author and teacher John Ortberg was starting his tenure at the groundbreaking megachurch Willow Creek, he called well-known philosopher-theologian Dallas Willard for advice. When asked how to stay unspoiled by the lures of the world and remain focused on growing spiritually, Willard's response was simple: "You must ruthlessly eliminate hurry from your life."

What would happen if we all ruthlessly eliminated hurry? That would mean reducing our schedules to significant activities and even then leaving some margin around those things we did schedule. It would mandate taking time to enjoy each of life's experiences, rather than just checking them off the to-do list and rushing to complete the next one. Because we would not be so preoccupied with a plethora of challenges, we would be free to give our undivided attention to each thing we did. Can you even imagine a life like that?

A simple life rearranges your thinking. For instance, meditation and reflection replace constant talk. Authenticity becomes more important than a polished image or a pristine appearance. You begin to focus more on developing your inner life rather than working on external conditions. A simple life finds value in beauty, purity, clarity, justice, and faith, rather than wealth, comfort, productivity, and consumption. Being a good citizen takes precedence over maximizing your individuality and fighting for your rights. Simplicity generates comfort in moderation rather than in excess, and it appreciates the mysteries of life rather than striving to solve them. Simplicity creates a desire to share what you have rather than hoarding what you can get. In the end, a simple life produces contentment in whatever circumstance you find yourself.

When my life was forcibly downshifted in prison, it was painful. At first I felt as if I was missing out on all the wonderful and important things that life had to offer. But I discovered an invaluable insight: if you invest in human connections rather than material consumption and productivity, your life is exponentially enriched. In other words, I was so much happier spending time getting to know the Lifers and sharing meaningful thoughts and experiences with them—even if the experiences themselves were forgettable—that I was no longer dying to get out.

One of the benefits of leading a simple life is the opportunity to experience balance. We have been designed to gain meaning and fulfillment by attending to needs in four key life dimensions: our emotional, physical, intellectual, and spiritual sides. Personally, reaching that sweet spot of satisfaction in each of those areas is exceedingly difficult when I allow myself to be victimized by other people's expectations and by a pace of activity determined by the world. Unfortunately, it's not unusual for me to completely ignore one or more dimensions because I have become so focused on a particular aspect of life (too often my work) that dominates my mind and heart.

So how does one begin to live the simple life? Consider San Quentin's rules of simplicity:

Don't worry about what you cannot change. Many inmates complained about injustice: how the courts misjudged them, how evil people get away with crimes, how certain laws make it impossible for people get a fair shake. One of the most difficult things about prison was entering with the belief that I was there without cause while others who should have been behind bars were allowed to walk free. Until I made peace with my circumstances, the time just dragged.

In the same way, people outside of prison wrestle with their own parcel of unrealistic concerns. Some stress over their kids getting into the right schools; some fret over their level of comfort. Others fear losing a job or not getting a promotion; still others worry about their retirement fund. Many of these pressures are self-induced and counterproductive. They are the very reason that Jesus told His students that we should not worry about everyday life since we cannot control those matters. But the One who can is always on task. If we concentrate on the things that matter—like loving and worshiping God, serving people, living godly lives, demonstrating the depth of our faith—then life becomes more manageable and far more pleasurable. The funny thing is that while the world says those things are secondary, Christ taught that they are the only things that actually matter (Matthew 6:25-34).

Redefine the things that bring fulfillment. Millions of people seem to derive both identity and fulfillment from the stuff they own. Whether it's the latest in mobile phones, PDAs, or MP3 players, higher-speed Internet connections, computers, or video games, the incessant drive to wrap our lives around such tools is often harmful. Our devotion to technology leaves us with less time for the things that are truly important. High-tech distractions capture our attention and energy, making us dependent upon them until we lose all sense of boundaries in other areas of our lives. When our possessions own us, we are waging a losing battle. We must learn to prioritize those things that bring us true fulfillment.

Align your life with the vision and abilities God has given you. Sometimes we spread ourselves too thin by pursuing too many things in too many different directions. That's why specifying the vision for your life—that desirable future that you believe God has gifted and called you to commit to—is critical. Once you can identify what that future is and build a strategy around it, it becomes possible to say no to what otherwise might seem like great opportunities. In reality, those alternatives may simply be a distraction from your ability to do the things that will give you the greatest fulfillment and produce the greatest results for the Kingdom of God. We need to be able to choose not what is good but what is *best*—which sometimes means saying no to the good things.

Be prepared to pay the price. Living a less complicated life breeds clarity of thought and better choices, but it can also make you a bit of an outsider. Think, for instance, about the Amish. Most Americans view them as quaint but odd. Some people feel sorry for them because they are so antiquated and "miss out" on so much that the world has to offer. Similarly, people who live within the mainstream world but embrace a simpler lifestyle are looked at askance. Simplicity can be a threat to those who are living a life legitimized by pop culture.

This might mean that your kids don't play every sport or participate in every activity that comes their way. You might not have the latest gadget, but you will be free to truly enjoy life and appreciate what you have.

Are you willing to try something radical, to experience the freedom that comes from living a simpler life? What steps do you need to take today toward making that happen?

TRANSFORMING PRINCIPLE
Make life simple.

CHAPTER 14

Find Freedom in Forgiveness

Inmates invariably have deep and difficult issues with forgiveness. Some need to seek forgiveness from those they have hurt. Others need to offer forgiveness to those who have hurt them. Most need both to give and to receive forgiveness if they ever hope to move on.

But forgiveness is not easy. Forgiveness requires us to surrender something without necessarily receiving anything in return. Forgiveness means giving up resentment, anger, pain, the desire for revenge, and the expectation of repayment or restoration, and that's tough to do, especially if those are the very things that provide the energy and purpose in our lives. But in San Quentin, I learned that until we release these negative feelings, we will forever be captive to them.

Forgiveness was the final, critical key to my own personal transformation. In order to be truly free, I still needed to deal with the unresolved anger in my heart: anger at God, anger at the dysfunctions of my past, anger at the business world for not being what I had hoped it would be. I was angry at the system for letting me down, angry at the COs and other inmates who tried to make my life miserable, and angry at myself for the poor choices I had made.

But the Lifers showed me that forgiveness was a necessary step in the process of transformation and restoration. Vy Le's journey through the path of forgiveness was both miraculous and instructive to me. From the first day Vy sat next to me in the chapel, I knew there was something different about him. He seemed to overflow with a peace and joy that were contagious. Vy's story of transformation was one of the most inspirational and compelling I had ever heard.

Vy had come to the United States from Vietnam when he was in his teens. He was one of the last people to safely emigrate before Saigon fell during the North-South conflict. His father had been a high-ranking official in the South Vietnamese government, so Vy had grown up relatively privileged in a beautiful house on the China Sea. But when the guerillas from the North invaded the South, Vy's father was brutally murdered and unceremoniously dumped in a local river. Vy's life was in danger, too, and he eventually fled the country just before the government collapsed.

Even years later, his struggle with those who had killed his father was especially challenging because he did not know who had done the killing and he would never have a chance to encounter them face-to-face. For many years, he burned inside with a hatred for those unknown assailants, finding it impossible to forgive them. That wasn't because it is impossible to forgive people without a confrontation but because the first step in any act of forgiveness is choosing to forgive.

Vy also had to deal with forgiveness over the kidnapping crime for which he was serving time. After his father was killed, Vy had come to the United States in search of a better life. But every effort he made to adapt to his new homeland seemed destined to failure. With little understanding of the language and the culture, he had difficulty holding down a job. He gave up on the American dream—for him, it had been one long nightmare—and surrounded himself with other immigrants from Vietnam.

One day, a group of Vy's new friends decided to kidnap a young girl from the home of a local Vietnamese family. Vy knew nothing of the plans until the crime had already occurred. Since the police would not be looking for Vy, his friends called and begged him to drive the car to pick up the ransom funds. Penniless and jobless at the moment, Vy was frustrated with the United States and life in general. His discouragement got the best of him, and he did what his housemates asked.

But by the time Vy had driven to the prearranged ransom drop, the police were waiting for him, and he was arrested. He was booked and placed in the county jail, and the authorities tried to get him to rat on his friends. But Vy was still steeped in his Vietnamese heritage and customs, and he refused to talk. Unfortunately, before the night was out, one of his "friends" ratted on him, making him out to be the brains behind the entire escapade. The actual mastermind of the crime copped a plea, contending that he had been just a minor player in the grand scheme that Vy had planned and led. As a result, the real ringleader was set free, serving no time at all. The others received short sentences. But Vy and two others were stuck holding the bag, each receiving a very long sentence. Vy was given seven years to life—a sentence that eventually would cost him twenty-three years of his life in prison.

Not surprisingly, Vy entered prison an angry young man. In the span of a few short years, he had lost his family to violence, been forced to leave his homeland, and gone from a lifestyle of privilege and comfort to one in which he struggled to survive. Convinced by the continual turn of hurtful events in his life that he could trust no one, his hostility produced a mean and menacing disposition.

While many people would have been emotionally broken by such a turn of events, the horrific circumstances simply fueled Vy's anger and commitment to fight back. Rather than give up on life, Vy found that he was energized by a promise he made to himself to kill the guy who had turned him in. Not an overly religious man, Vy nevertheless prayed every day that he would have a chance to get the revenge he thirsted for. He wanted only five minutes alone with the guy to repay him for ruining his life. He had no plan or even any idea how such vengeance might occur—after all, Vy was in prison and the ringleader was not—but he prayed that their paths would cross at some point. Vy was determined to be ready for that moment, and he played it over and over in his mind.

While he waited, his anger got him in trouble time after time. Finally, after one particular brawl, he was put in the Hole. But in ways that only God could orchestrate, Vy's time in the Hole was transformational. It was there that the God he'd been praying to for revenge met Vy. Even without a Bible or someone to preach to him, Vy experienced a miraculous conversion as God reached down to him in the lonely confines of the Hole, changed his heart, and transformed his life.

Once back in the mainline population at San Quentin, Vy turned his focus to more productive concerns, including life after parole. He started taking classes to better himself and spending time helping other inmates better themselves as well.

Unbeknownst to Vy, while God was helping him get his life on the right track, the kidnapping's ringleader—who had never done time for that crime—had since committed and been convicted of another felony. In the time that Vy had spent in the Hole and then taking classes to better himself, this guy had already completed his sentence in another California prison and then been shipped to San Quentin to wait out the final days of his term before he was paroled. (All California inmates spend their last few days in prison in that special section of San Quentin while their papers are processed.) Neither Vy nor the ringleader had any clue as to the whereabouts of the other.

One afternoon as Vy was returning to his cell, he passed by the reception area and something caught his eye. He paused to look inside the reception block cells and was stunned to see his nemesis sitting in a holding cell. At the same moment, the parole seeker caught Vy's eye and turned pale with fright.

Neither he nor Vy could move. They held each other's gaze for a few moments, until the shock wore off and reality set in.

Suddenly, just months after coming to grips with his anger and lust for revenge, Vy knew the moment of truth had arrived. Involuntary rage swept over him, and his instincts kicked into gear. He immediately returned to his cell to find a weapon—a shank that he had stashed under his bed. This was the moment he had prayed and dreamed about for so long. Despite his acceptance of Christ and the ways of God, this was a once-in-a-lifetime opportunity—perhaps even the gift from God that he had so faithfully prayed for. He was not going to squander his chance to get even and be forced to live the rest of his days with regret.

But what should have been a time of exhilarating anticipation instead crumbled into a time of emotional turmoil and confusion. Vy found that he was torn between his long-held desire for revenge and his newfound faith, which commanded him to be loving and forgiving. He walked around the prison for an hour, thinking about his choices and their implications.

Still perplexed, he took a detour to the chapel, where he began earnestly praying about what to do. While he was agonizing over his choices, one of the prison chaplains entered and could tell by the look on Vy's face that something was drastically wrong. Vy knew the chaplain well and trusted him, so he explained his dilemma. They talked about the pros and cons of taking revenge. Vy kept returning to the fact that since he had found peace with God, he wanted peace with the world as well. Revenge no longer seemed right. They prayed together, then talked some more.

Ultimately, Vy realized that deep down he wanted to do what was right and to arrive at a peaceful resolution, which could only happen if he faced his offender and forgave him. The chaplain offered to accompany him, but Vy knew he had to do this by himself on his own terms. He handed over the knife to the chaplain, who said he would dispose of the weapon.

With that, Vy left to face the man who had caused him so much pain and suffering. He made a beeline for the reception area, oblivious to the guards and other prisoners he passed en route. When Vy reached his tormentor's cell, he saw the man recoil in fear.

Vy entered the holding cell. The ringleader was frozen in place, standing just three feet away from a former friend whose life he had knowingly and carelessly destroyed. Looking his adversary square in the face, Vy moved closer and extended his right hand. The ringleader stood still, eyes fixed on the ground in shame and fright. Clearly, he was just waiting for the steel blade to pierce his skin and the life to ooze out of him.

Instead, Vy quietly spoke, "It is over now. I forgive you. You don't have to worry anymore. We must move on." Vy kept his hand extended, waiting to shake the hand of the man who had been his enemy for years. The other man was too stunned to react, perhaps assuming it was a trick to give Vy better position for the kill. He just stood there, avoiding eye contact, trembling, waiting for what he probably considered the inevitable fatal stabbing to take place.

A few more seconds passed. Vy repeated his words. The ringleader finally lifted his gaze, and his face bore a puzzled look. He made no effort to shake the hand of peace that had been extended to him. After more moments of silence ticked away, Vy turned around and walked out of the cell. He had accomplished what he came to do.

The power of forgiving this man transformed Vy forever. "God gave me back my life," he explained to me later. "He put me to the test, but He was faithful to me. When I left the cell after giving forgiveness, I felt alone at first. But then I felt a chill like a winter wind that rose up from underneath me. It went through my body, like a tingling. It really lifted me up. A large weight that had been on my shoulder for so long suddenly fell. I felt so light I wanted to jump. It took me many years to realize that a desire for vengeance just builds up more hatred. Finally, I was free of it all."

The final test came a few days later. Vy's antagonist was granted parole and walked through the gates a free man. Vy stayed behind bars for another sixteen years. But he felt comfortable with that turn of events, seeing it as a chance for God to get him fit for life beyond San Quentin. Although he badly wanted to go home, he understood that God was still molding him and getting him ready for life after prison.

For years Vy had been dragged down by his need to get even. But he found that it was forgiveness that provided his freedom, even while still living in San Quentin. "You cannot blame other people for your circumstances. You have to let it go. Otherwise, it controls you, it owns you, and you will never be really free. Your only hope is to forgive and move on."

III

Vy taught me and many others that when you forgive someone, the person offering forgiveness is the one who is released from bondage. When we extend forgiveness to the one who has hurt us, we are to expect nothing in return; the prize is our own freedom. Notice that the ringleader never extended any expression of apology, remorse, admission, or gratitude toward Vy. But when your heart is filled with the desire to forgive, a response is not necessary. The sense of peace that Vy felt while walking away from his forgiven adversary is the evidence that the bondage had been broken, and life could now proceed without the burden of negative emotions and desires that had held him hostage.

This philosophy is at the heart of the Christian faith. Naturally, Jesus' death and resurrection, His suffering for sins He did not commit in order that those who committed them could receive forgiveness, are the ultimate examples of extending grace. Many other biblical teachings emphasize the same lesson. The Lord's Prayer, for instance, describes our need to forgive others in order to receive forgiveness. Paul regularly instructed church leaders to encourage believers to demonstrate qualities such as love, kindness, compassion, and forgiveness. Jesus admonished people to create a lifestyle of forgiveness, telling Peter that he must forgive his offenders countless times, not just once or twice.

In every instance, forgiveness is a decision we make based on the principles of God's Kingdom rather than the standards of the world. When we follow His path, we experience greater levels of empathy, understanding, compassion, relief, and strength. Forgiveness enables us to become more like Christ.

The world, of course, has its own reasons for instigating forgiveness. The medical profession, for instance, has published numerous studies that extol the health benefits of forgiveness. Those include lower blood pressure, less stress, a better heart rate, decreased possibility of depression, reduced chronic pain, healthier relationships, a diminished likelihood of substance abuse, and more. Doctors believe in forgiveness because they know that it frees the body from the toxic effects of negative emotions and unproductive obsessions.

But the best reason to forgive is simply because we are indescribably thankful that God forgave us for offending Him without us asking for or deserving such grace.

Getting to the emotional and intellectual place where we are ready to forgive is no simple task. Often it takes time. Sometimes it requires us to understand the personal benefits, or at least to see how the refusal to forgive gnaws away at our hearts, minds, and souls.

Regardless of what it takes, I know forgiveness is possible because I watched it occur among the Lifers time after time. And I have personally experienced the life-giving power of letting go of the pain and negative emotions in favor of becoming an agent of peace and grace.

Is there anyone you need to forgive? It may take time for you to muster the courage to take that step. But the burden that will be removed from your life will set you free. Both you and the person to whom you extend such grace will never be the same.

Forgiveness is a choice. Ultimately, that choice is up to us. We can choose *not* to forgive, but that will only leave us in bondage. By choosing not to forgive, we are in essence choosing to remain in our own personal prisons. There were times in prison when I had to decide how I was going to deal with other people around me. I could choose either to be angry with them or to release them. Once I realized that it wasn't their actions but my attitude that was imprisoning me, it was much easier to forgive.

Offering forgiveness is a head rather than a heart action. You may not always *feel* like forgiving someone, but when you free that person in your head, you will eventually begin to feel it in your heart as the feelings follow the actions.

Forgiving is not necessarily forgetting. Although forgiveness is a crucial part of transformation, it doesn't mean that we need to set ourselves up to be hurt again. Sometimes there are people in our lives who are simply not good for us. We need to choose to forgive them for the hurts they have caused us, but also to set protective boundaries around our interactions with them. It *is* possible to forgive someone emotionally and mentally without opening ourselves up to more pain.

Forgiveness is a part of life. As long as we live on this earth, we will need to forgive others and to be forgiven. That means that at the same time we are offering forgiveness to others, they are extending grace to us. We are all human, and until we reach our eternal destination, we are all going to make mistakes. It's a simple fact of life.

TRANSFORMING PRINCIPLE
Forgiveness produces freedom.

CHAPTER 15

Life after Prison

Two months before my release date, the station manager at SQTV encouraged me to put together a résumé. It was the first time I even thought about the need to find a job on the outside. In the back of my mind I guess I was assuming that I would return to working with Young Life and maybe attend seminary in preparation for a career in ministry. But not having lined up anything, I decided Larry was right so I worked with him to compose a résumé. I then placed the finished document in a folder that I would take with me from prison.

Finally my release date arrived, and I was allowed to walk out the gates of San Quentin as a free man. I had grown and learned so much behind those walls, and I had developed such strong relationships with the people there, I was almost sad to go. But I was also full of hope.

And it was that hope that gave me a reason to climb out of bed each morning and set about doing what God planned for me to do. For the first time in my life, greatness was no longer about controlling the world; it was about honoring God by doing my small part in His unfolding plan. Success was no longer about flexing my intellectual or professional muscles in public; it was about deploying my inner strength to do what was right in every situation.

When I emerged from North Block, I really had nowhere to go. My homes were gone, and so was my former girlfriend. I moved into my parents' tiny one-bedroom apartment, where I slept on their living room floor. It wasn't the most comfortable situation but it was surprisingly bearable. I couldn't wait to replace my prison blues, but since I didn't have any money, my only option was old, outdated fashions. As a former clothing fanatic, you would have thought this would bother me. But it didn't. I was just thankful to have a roof over my head and clothes on my back.

I needed to find a job but had no car, so for months I rode the bus. Finally, Catholic Charities blessed me by giving me an old station wagon. It was hardly a chick magnet, but it got me to and from job interviews and my regular check-in meetings with my parole and probation officers.

Up close, my life wasn't too impressive. But the big picture was highly significant: I was happy, free, and looking forward to seeing what God had in store for me. I was not weighed down by credit card debt, an overwhelming schedule, unrealistic expectations, or the need to look a certain way or befriend cool people. Life was simple. Life was good.

In my free time—and I had more of it than I'd ever had before—I was able to ponder questions that most people don't seem to address. What was the purpose of my life? Was I doing what God made me to do? How was I adding value to the world? Was God being honored by my choices and who I was becoming? How could I develop relationships in ways that gave people the respect and dignity they deserved? What was God saying to me that I really needed to hear? There weren't any easy answers, but the growth that came from pursuing—and waiting for—those answers proved to be well worth the effort.

Living in the apartment eventually became claustrophobic for all of us, so I sought a new place to live. An acquaintance generously offered me the free use of a basement room in his home. That gave me the chance to look for a job and save up enough money to eventually rent a room in a house with three college students.

My expenses were minimal, but I still needed money for basic necessities. Getting a job was a little tougher than I had imagined. I pulled out the résumé Larry had helped me to create, and after a lot of searching, I strung together some part-time work with Young Life and the city's youth football and basketball teams. I prayed about working full-time with Young Life but sensed that it was not the right thing for me. Attending seminary was still an option, but that didn't seem right for me, either. Another possibility that emerged was working at a nearby television video production company owned by a Christian man I had met through Young Life. Eventually I decided to give that a try.

My first assignment at Television Associates—or

TVA—was telephone sales. Day after day I made calls to Silicon Valley tech companies trying to sell time in our editing suites. It was not the most exciting or fulfilling job, but it paid the bills and kept me in a business that I was familiar with from my days in prison. The people at TVA were kind, and I was grateful to have a job. Then, just as at SQTV, the boss started giving me more significant assignments. They ranged from generating new business opportunities to coordinating and producing shows. Once again, God paved the way for me to be intimately involved in an activity that was personally stimulating and that made use of the abilities He had invested in me.

The most spectacular part of this story, however, was yet to come. As I was becoming more integral to the workings of the company, I had one of those rare moments when God seemed to stop time and activity in order to fully capture my attention. On March 11, 1998, I believed God was telling me to start a satellite network that would deliver ministry training programs to churches around the country. Instead of a church sending several staff people to a conference—a very time-consuming, expensive process—they could put a satellite dish on the church building and have as many people as they wanted watch the programs that we beamed to their dishes. We could bring in the best teachers and trainers and reach a national audience of pastors and other church leaders— several times a month—for the same amount of money a church might spend to send staff to one conference a year.

I didn't know of any groups doing anything like that for the church, and it seemed like a winning idea.

Even though I was a bit hesitant about sharing the idea with Ed Carlstone, the owner of TVA, I decided to take the risk anyway and talk to him about it. Ed took the idea seriously and gave me invaluable direction for building the business, including ways to test the concept and decide if it had merit. I began working with two other men who would become great friends and trusted colleagues in the years to come. Reid Rutherford had an MBA from Stanford and was a successful businessman. He came alongside me and wrote the business plan. John Mumford was a highly regarded venture capitalist with an amazing track record and incredible wisdom and instincts. He provided the primary funding for the Church Communication Network (CCN) and continued to be a board member and treasured adviser on all of our endeavors.

Through this, God also seemed to be showing me something important about vocation: to maximize the joy I received, I had to be willing to trust Him enough to take some risks. There is a big difference between strategic risks and simply being reckless. But expanding to reach our full potential required us to step out in faith and try some things that took me outside of my comfort zone. After a lot of hard work to study the upsides and downsides and then to put the foundations in place, we aired our first program on CCN about a year after God first gave me the idea. Little did I know it at the time, but God would eventually allow our network to grow beyond our wildest dreams.

Today I am proud and humbled to serve as president of CCN and to have overseen the network's expansion from broadcasting a dozen programs a year to airing more than one hundred training programs and special ministry events every year. We also do numerous Web-based video-on-demand and live seminars and conferences in churches all over the country. The network has provided training and encouragement to more than a million people in ministry. All of this has been made possible because of CCN's outstanding group of Christian leaders and trainers, as well as our incredible staff. Those people will never know how much their professionalism, tireless effort, and personal support have meant to me. In essence, they have become my Lifers on the outside.

III

When I was released from prison in 1995, the fast lane beckoned me to come back and join the race. At that point, I was a completely different person than the Bill Dallas who had once surveyed the Bay Area and planned to take it over. Now I possessed a faith in Christ that had some depth, a life purpose that was not based on pillaging the land and its people, and a support system that was strong enough to show me the tough love I'd need to make it (even if that support was coming from a dozen or so convicted felons living behind bars). Despite those advantages, the temptation to jump back into the express lane to compete—to get the adrenaline rush and to return the focus to me—*was* appealing.

My early years out of prison were a stutter step of progress and regress. When breaks came my way I was always tempted to start believing the lie that it was all about me. Ambition, image, selfishness, arrogance—it all flashed before me, and I'd be lying if I said there weren't days when it was highly appealing.

But I'm fortunate to have had so many people in my life who helped me stay on track. Giving them access to my life and the authority to challenge me at any time was one of the best choices I ever made. In addition to spending time with friends from Young Life and my colleagues at TVA, I made monthly visits back to San Quentin to visit the Lifers, who were always more than happy to provide me with a good life check. Without any formal declarations or requests, the Lifers served as my life coaches by encouraging me and educating me as to how to maintain a proper life focus.

Years before I went to prison, I dated a girl named Toni, and together we had a son, Dallas. My relationship with Toni ended before Dallas was born, and although she didn't put any pressure on me to support Dallas, she did give me the option of being part of his life. Of course I said that was what I wanted. But before San Quentin, I hadn't ever really taken the time to develop any kind of deep relationship with him.

Dallas was eight years old when I went to prison, and when I was released, I couldn't wait to see him again. While I was behind bars, I realized what a privilege it was to be his father, and I couldn't wait to share my life with him. He became my number one priority, and I tried to spend as much time with him as I could.

One Sunday afternoon we were sitting in my old station wagon, and I turned to Dallas and said, "Son, I want you to know that I am in your life forever. Even if someone offered me a billion dollars to move across the country, I wouldn't even *think* about taking it. I will never leave you." After that, our relationship reached a whole new level. I thank God every day for the chance to be in Dallas's life and have him in mine.

In addition to this wonderful relationship with my son, God also blessed me with a wonderful wife, Bettina, who provided the breadth and depth of support that enabled me to keep growing. She became a constant source of stability, guidance, accountability, loyalty, grace—in short, the very epitome of love.

Even after leaving the thick walls of San Quentin, I never stopped learning life's lessons and applying the principles that I learned there. The very same principles that transformed me and helped me to cope with life when I was behind bars now serve as a springboard to living the very best life God has for me.

I embrace my trials. While I was in prison I wasted valuable, unrecoverable time fighting reality—a reality I could not change. I viewed my trial as an unfair intrusion in my life. Thankfully, the lightbulb eventually switched on, and I realized I could not transcend my problems until I embraced them as a means to a better future. Today, I can look at my time in San Quentin as the very best thing that ever could have happened to me because it was God's very best plan for my life. God used the "intrusion" of San Quentin to get my attention, reshape me, and make me into the man He intended me to become.

Jump forward fifteen years to my present life. Here I am, living on the other end of that hardship continuum. The joy I get to experience these days more than makes up for the trials He allowed me to go through. While I am far from perfect, my character has undergone substantial reconstruction—a work in progress, to be sure, but even the progress made has been a priceless gift. Bettina and I have a wonderful daughter, Amanda, and we live in a comfortable home on the coast of northern California. My relationship with Dallas continues to get better and better. I am blessed to serve the church through my amazing job at CCN. My work provides regular contact with many of the great Christian leaders, ministers, and teachers, as well as a variety of world-class business leaders, all of which is exciting and keeps me growing. Through those contacts I receive opportunities to minister directly to a variety of groups all across North America. And I am honored to lead a staff of people who work tirelessly, execute our plans superbly, and are a pleasure to work alongside day after day.

I cling to hope. Ever since leaving San Quentin, I've been enthusiastic about every new adventure I embark upon. By all rights, that should not be the case. When I left prison, I had no money. I would live the remainder of my life as a convicted felon. My girlfriend was long gone. I had no job and no job interviews lined up. I slept on a blanket on the floor in my parents' tiny apartment and drove a car with no heat. In some respects, my life appeared rather hopeless.

But I was alive! If you haven't hit bottom, you don't understand the significance of that statement. And I had gained an entirely new set of tools—self-respect, godly character, deeper moral convictions, substantive faith, supportive relationships, purpose, inner security, and life principles—to help navigate the rough waters.

Today I have hope for the future because I have hope in God. He's given me everything I need to handle the curves that life will inevitably throw at me.

I express myself through my work. Some people describe work as part of the Fall. But for me, work has always been a source of joy. And when I was in prison, it was also the source of healing, providing an outlet for my creativity and God-given abilities.

Although I no longer live in the fast lane, I still take great pleasure and satisfaction in my work at CCN. The main difference is that today I work for the glory of God rather than for my own selfish gains.

I choose sustaining faith. Once I got out of prison, I realized how easy it would be to grow lazy in my faith. I knew how to look the part of a Christian—I could attend church, give money, and memorize Scripture. But I also knew that if those outward expressions of faith didn't penetrate my heart, they would never sustain me through the inevitable storms of life.

Thankfully, the Lifers taught me that sustaining faith demands transformation, and such transformation can only be built on surrender, brokenness, and humility. Today I continue to walk very closely with God, constantly asking Him to be Lord of my life, to keep me focused on what is most important, and to lead me every step of the way.

I keep a proper self-image. While I was in San Quentin, my self-image underwent an extreme makeover. What is my self-image today? It has nothing to do with appearance, possessions, job title, or who I know. In my job as president of CCN, I work closely with many of the top Christian thinkers, communicators, and leaders of our time. But my value does not come from my association with these men and women of God. It comes from God Himself. My self-image is simply that I am a sinner forgiven by Christ, renewed daily by the Holy Spirit, and loved by a merciful God. I am a weak man who finds his strength in God and His Word, and who tries to bless his family, friends, and colleagues whenever possible. I try to live for an audience of one.

I reject self-absorption. During my monthly trips back to visit the Lifers at San Quentin, we always met in the general visitation hall, where I was able to watch the interaction between the short-timers and their family members. When a man goes to prison, if he has a wife and children, the primary (if not entire) burden for the welfare of the family usually is thrust upon the wife's shoulders. She becomes the mother, surrogate father, breadwinner, homemaker, educator, spiritual leader—you name it, she carries that responsibility alone.

Watching the interplay between those strong women and their selfish husbands always got my blood boiling, especially when the husband was still so focused on his own discomfort and insecurities that he barely paid attention to the state of the wife and children he'd left behind. I would watch these fatigued, heartbroken women coming all the way to prison to see their mates, only to find that these men were visiting with them in body but not in spirit. Their self-absorption had already irreparably harmed their families when they went off to prison, and these men continued to injure their families by robbing their wives of even a few hours of respite, encouragement, and gratitude. It was common for those reunions to end in heated, angry conversations.

The reunions of the Lifers with their family and friends, however, had a totally different tenor. The focus of those conversations was almost exclusively on the visitors. Those interactions were peaceful and relaxed. I didn't have to eavesdrop to figure out that these inmates were busy giving of themselves to those who had come to see them.

Even today I feel sad when I consider how much attention I showered on myself during my first couple of years in prison. What a pompous fool I was to devalue the efforts and emotions of my mother, my stepfather, my girlfriend, and the handful of others who went out of their way to visit me and lift my spirits. I ignored the pain and needs of other inmates in order to bore them with the details of my own circumstances. In the end, everybody lost out because of my insistence on making every conversation about Bill Dallas. Recognizing that I will never be able to recapture that lost time and, in a few instances, the relationships that dissolved because of my self-absorption makes me even more determined to keep my focus on God and others, and off myself.

I shape my attitude. When I emerged from San Quentin, I discovered that those dysfunctional-family tapes that had played so often in my mind while I was growing up were still operational, even after a few years of silence. Here I was, an ex-con, starting from scratch in my midthirties, living in modest conditions, unable to find a suitable job.

Would I really trust the principles I had learned in San Quentin? Perhaps I was afraid to succeed. Having lived in the midst of fear and failure for so long, it was all I knew. In a strange way, it was my comfort zone. I felt as if I did not deserve to do well. It seemed that I needed to continue to pay a debt to society, and that included not rising above others or doing anything too visible or significant. What right did I have to try again?

But shortly after getting settled, a friend I met at church sensed my struggle and shared a statement from South African leader Nelson Mandela, himself a prisoner who perhaps struggled with the same issue that plagued me. It read: "Our deepest fear is not that we're inadequate. Our deepest fear is that we are powerful beyond measure. It is our light, not our darkness, that most frightens us. We ask ourselves, who am I to be brilliant, gorgeous, talented, and fabulous? Actually, who are you not to be? You are a child of God. Your playing small doesn't save the world. There is nothing enlightened about shrinking so that other people won't feel insecure around you."

That wisdom, along with recognizing how much I had overcome in prison through God's grace and guidance, has helped me change my attitude about my God-given calling and potential. It is one fear that I have been able to overcome. And you, too, have a God-given calling. I guarantee it.

I give respect. Having stripped me of every possession and accomplishment that previously defined me, prison taught me the importance of real respect: both giving and receiving it. I learned that each person has value—whether a billionaire, a celebrity, or an inmate. We all deserve respect simply because of our innate value as human beings, not because of our status or accomplishments.

I persevere until I "get it." Starting up CCN was not always easy, and I thought of giving up more than once. There was a point in June of 1999 when we were struggling to get the funding we needed and the business didn't seem to be getting much traction. It seemed as if we would never make it off the ground, and I was very discouraged. But San Quentin had taught me the importance of persevering. Even though we weren't making any visible progress, I just knew that I needed to hold on. And thankfully I did, because today CCN is a thriving ministry that reaches the hearts of people all over the world. Ten years before my San Quentin experience, I would not have been able to continue in the face of such dismal odds.

I let life come to me. San Quentin taught me to take life one day at a time. As much as we try, we can never really force the important things: time, relationships, faith. I've learned not to cut corners if I want to enjoy the full experience. By allowing God to orchestrate my life according to His plan rather than my own, I've learned to really enjoy this journey.

I live simply. One of the benefits of life in prison was the lack of distractions and choices. Because most of our options and factors that might distort our focus were removed, it was easy to think clearly and make good decisions. Thankfully, the absence of distractions within prison enabled me to grasp the wisdom of the psalmist who wrote about God instructing His people to "be still, and know that I am God" (Psalm 46:10).

But the success of CCN has driven home another lesson for me: the busyness and pressures of worldly success can quickly crowd out the principles that fostered the success in the first place. Titles, strong emphasis on the bottom line, implementing creative ideas and solutions, hiring a large team, initiating technological breakthroughs, associating with well-known and respected people—all of those are exactly the kind of distractions that pull me away from living a more simple and focused life. In a way, I could easily find myself right back in a situation similar to that which sent me to San Quentin. So I intentionally try to maintain a slower pace of life.

When things get too busy I'm more likely to lose perspective. When my daily agenda is less cluttered and slower paced, I am able to see myself more accurately. Slowing down is not easy, especially for a type triple A personality. But I know from experience that the positives far outweigh the negatives. Today I scour my schedule and try to figure out how to eliminate even one-quarter of the activities that are not necessary so that I can focus more directly on what matters and see things in the right context.

I find freedom in forgiveness. One of the most important lessons the Lifers of San Quentin taught me is this: anger toward others is a sentence more devastating than any judge could ever render. The only way we can break those shackles of anger and pain is to exercise complete and utter forgiveness.

Even when I might not feel it in my heart, I know that true forgiveness is an active, intentional choice on my part. And when I take that first step in choosing to forgive, I am finally able to live in true freedom.

III

On a plane ride to the East Coast recently, I found myself sitting near William H. Macy, the actor best known for movies such as *Fargo, The Cooler, Wild Hogs*, and *Seabiscuit*. I was working on the notes for this book but stopped for a few moments to watch him read through a screenplay. It brought to mind my college days when I studied theater and dreamed of becoming an actor. That, of course, never happened (although some of my pre-prison business exploits amply demonstrated the proficiency of my acting skills).

I wondered for a few minutes what might have happened if I had moved to Los Angeles or New York after graduation and pursued an acting career. But the principle of letting life come to me—as it is best designed for me—quickly redirected my thought pattern. God knew that I needed the San Quentin experience to become a man of character and a person He could use to advance His Kingdom. Maybe He would have engineered a similar outcome if I had entered the entertainment industry. Regardless, there is no looking back and no regrets. I am thrilled with where God has me today.

I don't know where He'll lead me tomorrow. All that matters is that I allow Him to direct my steps and that I make the most of the opportunities He provides me. I know I need to stay in the game, because the best is yet to come!

CHAPTER 16

He Was Always in Control

My story could not have been concocted by Hollywood; it includes too many bizarre twists and strange occurrences for it to be believable. But as I close out my reflections on this portion of God's investment in my life, let me tell you one of the most striking episodes from that period of my life.

It happened a year after I had gotten out of prison. By that time, I had a steady job providing a regular paycheck. I was living on my own in a place I could afford. I was no longer part of the fast-lane crowd; I was supporting myself, advancing in my relationship with God, and building a new life. Best of all, I was content.

During my quiet time alone with God one morning something very unique and special happened: I heard the still, small voice of God speaking to me. As much as I'd like to hear that voice on a regular basis, it happens only on rare occasions. But that particular morning, the voice was clearly reminding me of 4-N-10. As I considered that, I wasn't sure what to make of it. But then I thought more about 4-N-10.

You may recall that when I entered San Quentin, my first cell was on the fourth tier in North Block—specifically, 4-N-10. There was nothing particularly noteworthy about that cell. I lived in that space for a short while, adjusting to life in San Quentin before being relocated to another cell. Before I was paroled, I lived in more than ten different cells and dorm situations. This was normal for prisoners. We knew never to get too comfortable because everything could change in a minute. The message was clear: we didn't control the circumstances.

In the waning days before my parole, I was moved one last time: back to 4-N-10.

4-N-10!

God brought me to San Quentin and placed me in 4-N-10 on my very first day, and when He took me out of prison on my very last day, He did so from 4-N-10. The journey had come full circle. God used prison to accomplish what needed to be done in my life. I had entered as a broken, hopeless, self-absorbed, shallow person. I had fought with God, begging Him not to make me enter that cell. Was He indeed a God who loved me? If so, then where was He? Why wasn't He involved? Didn't He see my pain? Didn't He care?

Now I had my answer. I left 4-N-10 as a humbled, hopeful, growing servant of God. Without my seeing it, He had been there. He had been in control all along.

He always was. He always will be.

Think about it. The probability of me entering and leaving from the same cell is infinitesimally small. And it was not a coincidence. As with everything in my life—and yours—that event was carefully designed and executed by God. He is a God of details, even in the process of resurrecting shattered lives.

I was sent to prison because of my own choices, but I went to San Quentin as part of God's *perfect choice* for my life. It all seemed so wrong to me. I had lost all hope and had no clue as to how I would ever survive this ordeal. It did not seem possible that anything positive could emerge from that experience. At that time, life after prison was the furthest thing from my mind; there was no reason to believe that I would live that long.

I came into prison because I had done things my way. I left prison determined to do things God's way. Certainly I fought it sometimes, but eventually I realized that I am always better off when I surrender to Him and embrace the changes He introduces.

When I left San Quentin, I was mentally, physically, emotionally, and spiritually fit—in the best shape of my life in each of those dimensions. I had been excited about life before it crashed, but it had been the excitement of the chase, the notion that I could take the world by force, on my terms. The excitement I felt when leaving San Quentin was different. It was a peaceful, calm anticipation about the good things to come, knowing that any success experienced would be a gift from God. For the first time, my future was not about me or what I orchestrated to achieve my goals. I left San Quentin a healthier person.

In His own way and timing, God had transformed my life. He used the most unexpected of circumstances, places, and people to facilitate that renaissance. Nobody could have scripted a more unusual—or more effective—turnaround for me. I was in the midst of it, and I didn't see it coming until it was too late to stop it. God's love is like a freight train on a deadline: You cannot stop it, you cannot redirect it. You only know that it will deliver the goods as promised. But it wasn't until that morning, a year later, sitting on my bed with a Bible in my lap and a cup of Folgers at my side, that I saw how God perfectly and fittingly closed that chapter of my life. I had been so busy during those last few weeks inside the walls of San Quentin—saying good-bye to people I loved, completing paperwork for the administration, finishing the edits on a series of video projects I had begun for SQTV—that I missed the delicate and deliberate handiwork of God in the final moments.

Today, Bill Dallas is still a work in progress, but there is reason to believe I am now on the right track. The miracle that God initiated in my life is the same kind of reconstruction He wants to do with each of us. If you let Him, He will do amazing, unfathomable things in you and through you. His ways are not your ways, and He sees things you do not see, so the track to wholeness is not always what you might expect or desire. It is simply what's best—for you. The choice to cooperate or contest His work is up to you. I heartily recommend cooperating. And know this: even when you don't fully cooperate, He still is in control and will change your life for the better.

So wherever you are today, know that God loves you very much. He loves you so much that He will do whatever it takes for you to become the complete person He designed you to be.

Rest assured, He will use the trials and circumstances of your life to accomplish that goal. He never starts anything significant in your life just to leave it unfinished. He loves you too much for that.

Whether you've not yet faced tough times or you are going through some tough times right now, you can trust that He will use the circumstances of your life to your very best advantage. The journey won't always be easy, but rest assured, the ending will be spectacular.

Endnotes

1. A. W. Tozer, *The Root of the Righteous* (Harrisburg, PA: Christian Publications, 1955).

2. Rick Warren, *The Purpose Driven Life* (Grand Rapids, MI: Zondervan, 2002), 67.

3. National surveys by The Barna Group, a marketing research firm in Ventura, California, indicate that although 83 percent of the adult population describe themselves as Christian, just 22 percent say their relationship with God or Jesus Christ is the most important relationship in their lives. Also, fewer than one out of every five say they have a deep and intimate relationship with God today. For more information about Americans' spiritual condition, visit http://www.barna.org; also, see *Revolution* by George Barna (Carol Stream, IL: Tyndale House, 2005).

4. David Crary, "Record-High Ratio of Americans in Prison," *USA Today*, February 28, 2008.

5. These statistics are from The Barna Group and are based on its national tracking studies of lifestyles and attitudes. These tracking surveys interview a minimum of one thousand adults based on a national sample of people eighteen or older. For more information, visit http://www.barna.org.

6. Ibid.

Discussion Guide

Chapters 1–2

1. What challenges in your life have made you feel like you were living in "prison" and separated from the love and power of God?

2. What are some common ways that people try to fill the "God-shaped" vacuum in their lives? What are some of the ways that you personally have attempted to fill that vacuum?

3. When Bill Dallas became a Christian after listening to the television preacher, he did everything right: he prayed, memorized Scripture, and attended church faithfully. But in spite of all this activity, his spiritual roots were still quite shallow. Why is that? What was missing in his foundation of faith?

4. Bill Dallas believes that being sentenced to San Quentin was no accident, that it was all part of God's best plan for his life.

What were the "coincidences" that had to occur in order for him to end up in San Quentin? Do you believe these were God orchestrated? Why?

Chapters 3–4

1. Do you believe that God has a plan for each person's life? If so, how do you see this playing out in your own life?

2. Do you embrace or run from trials? What are some of the ways that trials can be stepping-stones to a better life? What trials have you faced that ultimately led you to a better life?

3. What do you think causes people to lose hope? Where do you find hope when life seems most hopeless?

4. When you feel hopeless, what kinds of things help you hang on until you find hope again?

5. What is one thing you can do this week to practice the principles of embracing trials and hanging on until hope returns?

Chapters 5–6

1. What is your attitude toward work? Do you consider it a blessing or a curse? Why?

2. Have you found your own sweet spot? What particular skills and abilities has God gifted you with? How might you use these gifts to express yourself and serve Him best?

3. Bill Dallas viewed Christianity as a set of impossible standards that he could never meet no matter how hard he tried.

To what extent do you relate to his experience? What lessons did he learn in San Quentin that changed his perspective? How did these lessons affect your perspective?

4. What's the difference between empty religion and sustaining faith?

5. Wherever you are on your faith journey, what steps might you take to move toward a stronger faith?

Chapters 7–8

1. How would you describe your current self-image? What role do your career, talents, appearance, and financial well-being (or lack thereof) play in determining how you feel about yourself? What role does God play in the way you view yourself?

2. What can you do this week to begin seeing yourself the way God does? What help will you need?

3. Why is it sometimes so difficult to take your eyes off yourself and instead focus on God and others?

4. Why is it important to focus on your character rather than on your circumstances? What are some practical ways to do that when circumstances are especially difficult?

5. In chapter 8, Bill Dallas lists six questions that he recommends each of us ask ourselves to get a clearer picture of where we really focus our attention. In a notebook or journal, write down those questions and answer them for yourself. What did you notice or learn from the experience?

Chapters 9–10

1. What "attitude derailers" do you struggle with the most?

2. Where in your life do you need an attitude adjustment? Look at the list of suggestions at the end of chapter 9. Which of these steps toward developing a new attitude do you want to apply this week? What help will you need?

3. Describe a time when you felt that someone did not give you the respect you deserved. How did you feel?

4. Describe a time when you felt that someone gave you *more* respect than you felt you deserved. How did *that* feel?

5. In what ways do you sometimes fail to give others the respect they deserve? How does disrespect for others diminish your own dignity?

Chapters 11–12
1. Describe a time when you felt like giving up. What did you do?

2. Where do you find the strength to persevere when you feel like giving up?

3. What good things come from persevering through difficulty?

4. When things don't go your way, does it ruin your day or do you accept it as a minor disruption? Do you find it easy or difficult to let life come to you? Why?

5. How do letting life come to you and living in the moment draw a person closer to God?

Chapters 13–14

1. What areas of your life need simplifying? Does technology help or hinder your spiritual journey? Explain.

2. What steps can you take this week to "ruthlessly eliminate hurry from your life"?

3. How can the lack of forgiveness imprison you?

4. Is there someone in your life you need to forgive today? What would it take for you to do so? How might doing so benefit you?

Chapters 15–16

1. When Bill Dallas reflects on his life he can see how God has been at work in *all* his circumstances—good and bad. Reflecting on your life journey, how have you seen God at work?

2. Reflect on the principles in *Lessons from San Quentin*. Which do you need to apply in your life today? What help will you need?

About the Authors

Bill Dallas is the CEO of the Church Communication Network (CCN), a satellite and Internet communications company serving thousands of churches across North America. He hosts *Solutions*, a weekly satellite program with Dr. Henry Cloud and Dr. John Townsend. A former Young Life leader and Bible study teacher, Bill is a graduate of Vanderbilt University in Nashville. He is the proud father of Dallas and Amanda. Bill and his wife, Bettina, live in northern California.

George Barna is the founder and directing leader of The Barna Group, Ltd., a California-based company that offers primary research and strategic assistance related to cultural assessment and transformation, faith dynamics, and leadership development. He writes the popular biweekly *Barna Update* regarding his current research related to faith and cultural dynamics, available at http://www.barna.org. To date, Barna has written more than forty books, including the best sellers *Revolution*, *Transforming Children into Spiritual Champions*, *The Frog in the Kettle*, and *The Power of Vision*. He has been married to his wife, Nancy, since 1978 and has three daughters, Samantha, Corban, and Christine.

>Books by George Barna

Committed, born-again Christians are exiting the established church in massive numbers. Why are they leaving? Where are they going? And what does this mean for the future of the church? In this groundbreaking book, George Barna examines the state of the church today—and compares it to the biblical picture of the church as God intended it to be.

How can parents make a lasting impact on the spiritual lives of their children? To find the answer, George Barna researched the lives of thriving adult Christians and discovered the essential steps their parents took to shape their spiritual lives in childhood. *Revolutionary Parenting* shows parents how to instill in their children a vibrant commitment to Christ.

Many Christians take it for granted that their church's practices are rooted in Scripture. Yet how do our practices compare to those of first-century believers? *Pagan Christianity?* leads us on a fascinating tour through history that examines and challenges every aspect of the present-day church experience.

BARNA